LIVING IN UNION WITH CHRIST IN TODAY'S WORLD

Living in Union with Christ in Today's World

THE WITNESS OF
John CALVIN
and
IGNATIUS *Loyola*

Conference Papers from
St Patrick's College, Maynooth

Edited by Brendan McConvery

VERITAS

Published 2011 by
Veritas Publications
7–8 Lower Abbey Street
Dublin 1
Ireland
publications@veritas.ie
www.veritas.ie

ISBN 978 1 84730 265 6

Copyright © Brendan McConvery and the individual
contributors, 2011

10 9 8 7 6 5 4 3 2 1

The material in this publication is protected by copyright law.
Except as may be permitted by law, no part of the material may
be reproduced (including by storage in a retrieval system) or
transmitted in any form or by any means, adapted, rented or
lent without the written permission of the copyright owners.
Applications for permissions should be addressed to the
publisher.

A catalogue record for this book is available from the British
Library.

Designed by Lir MacCárthaigh, Veritas
Printed in Ireland by Hudson Killeen, Dublin

*Veritas books are printed on paper made from the wood pulp
of managed forests. For every tree felled, at least one tree is
planted, thereby renewing natural resources.*

CONTENTS

Remembering John Calvin and Ignatius Loyola at Maynooth

Brendan McConvery

John Calvin, one of the major figures of the Reformation, was born in 1509. The five hundredth anniversary of his birth was marked in the worldwide Reformed tradition by conferences, publications and other events. St Patrick's College, Maynooth, may have seemed an unlikely venue in which to celebrate such a central figure of the Reformed tradition, but a conference on 8-9 October, 2010, brought together scholars, pastors and laity from the Reformed, Roman Catholic and other traditions in Ireland for a weekend of conversation and fellowship. The title of the conference, *Living in union with Christ in today's world: the contribution of John Calvin and Ignatius Loyola*, sought to highlight the continuing relevance of these two teachers of the Gospel, not just for the members of their own communities, but for the whole of God's people today.

College days often throw unlikely people together. The precocious seventeen-year-old John Calvin was nearing the end of his studies at the Collège de Montaigu of the University of Paris, the Sorbonne, and planning to study law at the University of Orléans when an older student arrived. He was a thirty-five-year-old Basque ex-soldier, Iñigo (better known later as Ignatius) de Loyola who had undergone a conversion experience some thirteen years previously while recovering from wounds received at the battle of Pamplona. Eighteen years older than Calvin, Loyola had to struggle hard to acquire enough of a classical and philosophical grounding to enable him to embark on theological studies at the Sorbonne. Whether they were aware of one another's presence in the college, we do not know. In later years their ways diverged sharply. It is appropriate that Maynooth should be the place for an encounter commemorating two such contrasting figures, since it traces its theological pedigree as an institution of learning to the Sorbonne, some of whose émigré professors, forced into exile by the French Revolution, formed the core of its first teaching staff.

Discovering the riches of common traditions, not to mention those of unfamiliar ones that have often seen themselves as competitors, or at times even locked in bitter rivalry, demands careful and scholarly exploration. It is my first duty as editor to record a debt of thanks to the contributors of the papers in this volume for the scholarly, yet highly accessible, way in which they take us on a tour of the complex, and sometimes fraught, careers of both Calvin and Loyola.

Many others shared in the work of preparation for the conference and deserve to be mentioned here. Monsignor Hugh Connolly and Dr Trevor Morrow acted as joint hosts of the event. Mgr Connolly made the facilities of the College available to us with great generosity and kindness. The catering and accommodation departments of Maynooth College cared for our physical needs with their usual courtesy and good humour. Mrs Penny Woods, librarian of the Russell Library, the college's specialist collection, assembled a collection of material from the early Reformation period whose richness surprised and delighted many. In addition to Mgr Connolly and Dr Morrow, conference sessions were chaired by Dr Keith

McCrory, Fr Gerry Reynolds and Rev. Lorraine Kennedy-Ritchie. A preparatory committee met frequently in the months leading up to the conference. Its members included Revs Ivan Hull, Keith McRory, Tom Wilson, Gordon Campbell, Gerry Reynolds and Ken Newell. Kevin Hargaden was our technical expert who, among many other services, set up and maintained the conference website, recorded the lectures and, with the help of his friends in the Maynooth Community Church, managed the conference bookings. Gerard Fitzsimons of NUIM Computer Centre transposed into text form the audio file of the lively workshop led by Rev. Tom Wilson and Fr Tom Layden SJ. Postgraduate students from the Faculty of Theology in Maynooth rendered valuable service in welcoming and greeting our guests.

Veritas Publications responded with alacrity to a very tentative proposal to prepare the papers of the conference for publication.

A very deep debt of gratitude is due to two men whose sense of the Gospel and its call drives all they do and provided the inspiration for this conference. Ken Newell has a distinguished career as a Presbyterian minister behind him, including a year as Moderator of the General Assembly (2004–2005). His retirement from his ministry in the Fitzroy congregation in Belfast gave him some time to come up with the idea of bringing such unlikely companions as Calvin and Loyola together. In doing so, as in many other projects over the years, he was abetted by Fr Gerry Reynolds C.Ss.R. of Clonard Monastery. Ken and Gerry have a lively sense that the churches must cherish and learn from one another's prophets, saints and teachers and this was the inspiration that guided this conference. They also have a charm that it is impossible to resist and a spirit of faith which, if it does not exactly move mountains, moves even more intractable objects such as the minds and hearts of academics to commit themselves to a common project such as this. It is with something of that spirit that these papers are presented to a wider audience in the hope that we need no longer see John Calvin and Ignatius Loyola as opponents but as two people, living in difficult times but passionate for Christ, his Gospel, his Church and his mission and from whom still we have much to learn.

Brendan McConvery C.Ss.R.
St Patrick's College
Maynooth

Chapter i

Living in Union with Christ according to John Calvin (1509–1564)

Stephen N. Williams

When the name of Calvin is spoken, what are its popular associations? Three come to mind. Firstly, Calvin taught a hard-line doctrine of predestination. Secondly, he was fiercely anti-Catholic. Thirdly, he ran a tyrannical regime in Geneva. Before we take the plunge into Calvin, it is as well to say a brief word on the first two of these scores; we shall take longer on the third, as this will give us an appropriate entrée into Calvin.

Firstly, with respect to predestination, 'hard-line' is a value judgement and one that may be warranted. It is important, however, to remember that Calvin did not regard himself as the historical initiator of this teaching in the history of the Christian Church, and a study of medieval teaching on predestination brings to light its precedents. Calvin owed much to Augustine, although just how much is a matter for discussion, and Calvin certainly called no man master. As he interpreted Augustine, he was substantially reproducing his developed thought when he taught that the fate of individuals, whether bliss or perdition, was a matter of God's sovereign decision. Augustine stands as a towering figure behind both the Catholic and the Protestant traditions which have appropriated him. As far as Calvin's thought is concerned, those of us who stand in the Presbyterian tradition feel free as a matter of principle to agree or disagree with him on the question of predestination and, as a matter of fact, a range of views has long existed in the Presbyterian tradition, although the various Confessions of the Reformed Churches typically circumscribe these quite strictly and this admittedly qualifies the freedom of principle.

Secondly, with respect to Calvin's anti-Catholicism, it is indeed fair to characterise him in that way. His work is often plundered in order to garner his sentiments on the Roman Catholic Church and more favourable sentiments are frequently mined and quoted, but his indictment was undoubtedly severe.[1] What were his criteria? The logic of this strand of Reformation reasoning seems to be particularly well illustrated in the case of Heinrich Bullinger, the influential successor of another Reformer in Zurich, Huldrych Zwingli. It looks as though Bullinger, in trying to form his mind on the issues that divided Catholics and Protestants, found himself driven from the medieval theologians to the Fathers, whom the medievals regarded as authoritative, and from the Fathers to Scripture, which the Fathers regarded as authoritative, thus arriving at the principle that Scripture is the criterion according to which we make theological all judgements.[2] Exercising his judgement accordingly, Bullinger found in favour of Protestantism, rather than Catholicism, and this was precisely the ground of Calvin's conviction. Like Bullinger, he was very attentive to the Church

---

1. See the concluding section of the second chapter of the fourth book of the *Institutes of the Christian Religion*, volume 2, tr. F.L. Battles (Westminster: Philadelphia, 1960), 1052–53, which I take to be a representative, though not an exhaustive, account of Calvin's position. From now on, reference will be made to section, rather than page, numbers in this and the first volume.

2. See B. Gordon and E. Campi, *Architect of Reformation: An Introduction to Heinrich Bullinger, 1504–1575* (Grand Rapids: Baker Academic Press, 2004).

Fathers and believed that the medieval Catholic Church had moved away from them in significant respects. So eager was Calvin to maintain what continuity he could with the Fathers, although he himself did not favour episcopacy as a form of Church government, he defended the Fathers' decision to adopt it in their own time.[3] But he did not hesitate to depart from them either, if he judged that they deviated from Scripture. The reasoning behind Calvin's anti-Catholicism, was that the Catholic Church had, from a formal point of view, departed from an adequate principle of biblical authority and, from a material point of view, departed from an adequately biblical theology.

Thirdly, are we speaking of a tyrant? There is no need for anyone to defend everything that Calvin was and did. Calvin spoke of himself as, by nature, inclined towards 'modesty, softness, mildness' and self-critically added that he was timid and cowardly in disposition.[4] His successor as leader in Geneva, Theodore Beza, who greatly admired Calvin, admitted that his colleague and predecessor was hot-tempered and could be 'gloomy and difficult'.[5] If these characterisations are accurate, we are bound to wonder whether Calvin over-compensated for these traits, for it was undoubtedly characteristic of him to refuse to brook opposition.[6] To evaluate the extent to which his regime

---

3. *Institutes* IV.iv.2–4.

4. B. Cottret, *Calvin: A Biography* (Edinburgh: T&T Clark, 2000), xi. The most recent scholarly biography of Calvin is that of Bruce Gordon, *Calvin* (New Haven: Yale University Press, 2009) but those wanting a less detailed introduction will profit from older accounts such as those of F. Wendel, *Calvin: The Origins and Development of His Religious Thought* (London: Collins, 1963) and various accounts by T.H.L. Parker, such as John Calvin (Berkhamsted: Lion, 1975).

5. Cottret, *Calvin*, 4.

6. This comes out particularly strongly in Gordon.

should be called 'tyrannical', it would be necessary to work our way scrupulously through all its varied features.[7] Without wishing either to exculpate Calvin entirely or to endorse this picture of him, let me indicate another side to Calvin, quite deliberately picking out those positive features of which those who hear his name are usually unaware.

Born in Noyon, France, in 1509, son of a father who succeeded quite well in the world of financial and legal administration, Calvin's early studies took him to Paris and Orléans where they became directed towards the legal profession, rather than to the priesthood, as was originally intended. His conversion from Catholicism to the position of the Reformed churches is something on which he commented very sparingly, but we learn that it took place in 1533 (although Calvin could also describe it in terms of a more protracted period). His alliance with the Reformed cause took him to Switzerland, specifically to Geneva, with a period in Strasbourg in between two ministries in Geneva. It is the second of these Genevan ministries that was the making of Calvin as the leader of a new epoch and he remained there from 1541 to his death. Exercising leadership was bound to be difficult for a Frenchman in Switzerland, a land whose civil and ecclesiastical politics were complicated. Working in what was an often uneasy alliance with the civil authorities, Calvin, as

---

7. Intellectual historians may find it intriguing that, in *The Social Contract*, Rousseau makes the observation that '[t]hose who think of Calvin only as a theologian know very little of the full extent of his genius. Our wide edicts, in the framing of which he played a large part, do him no less honour than his *Institutes*. Whatever changes time may bring to our religious observances, so long as the love of country and of liberty is a living reality with us, the memory of that great man will be held in veneration.' See *Social Contract: Essays by Locke, Hume, Rousseau*, introduced by Ernest Barker (Oxford: Oxford University Press, 1971), 206, n. 8.

a teacher and leader of the Church, instituted a Presbyterian form of church government in Geneva which had espoused Protestantism.[8]

What is not widely known at the popular level is the passion and extent of Calvin's commitment to social transformation and justice. Not only did he appoint deacons whose specific job was to care for the sick and the poor, he personally promoted the cause of the general hospital in Geneva, established in 1535 to care for orphans as well as the sick and the poor. When there were food shortages amongst the many refugees in Geneva, Calvin combated both greed and poverty. He sought to eliminate beggary in Geneva because he wanted to guarantee the maintenance of every person in the city. The city was apparently the site of the first compulsory primary schooling in Europe. Working hours were restricted and Sunday was made into a holiday from work, although it was to be used for worship and spiritual edification. Where Calvin did not actually inaugurate these initiatives, he maintained and expanded them. Welfare medicine, apprenticeship in trade, provision of employment where people were otherwise unable to practise their craft, the development of the weaving industry, increasing the wages of teachers, protecting the hospital poor against cruelty and neglect – all these were Calvin's concerns, joined to the pursuit of a very simple lifestyle for himself. He preached over two hundred times from the book of Deuteronomy in the last decade of his ministry, frequently using it as a basis for chastising both landlords for charging high rents and magistrates for not judging impartially.

---

8. What this means is described in *Institutes* IV.iii.

The heartbeat of Calvin's theology is easily monitored when we study his ministry in Geneva. He regarded zeal for the glory of God as the proper centre of all feeling, thought and endeavour, and the whole of personal, ecclesial and civic life must be ordered to that end. In this respect, Calvin's spirit is well displayed in Abraham Kuyper, Prime Minister of the Netherlands from 1901–1905 and renowned before that as founder of the Free University of Amsterdam. The cosmic lordship of the triune God, exercised through Jesus Christ, was Kuyper's passion. 'There is not a square inch in the whole domain of our human existence over which Christ, who is Lord of all, does not say: "Mine".'[9] That is quintessential Calvinism. Kuyper's development of Calvin's legacy is, in fact, one of the most important developments in Reformed thought since the sixteenth century, although widely neglected in the English-speaking world outside of North America and controversial in its precise connection with Calvin's own thought. Calvin's theology of divine glory was as christocentric as it was theocentric, and it will function as a helpful bridge into the main portion of our discussion if we quote his comment on Paul's association of the glory of God and the person of Christ when he speaks of 'the glory of God in the face of Jesus Christ' (2 Cor 4:6). According to Calvin, this is

> ... an important passage from which we may learn that God is not to be sought after in His inscrutable majesty (for he dwells in light inaccessible) but is to be known in so far as He reveals Himself in Christ ... It is more profitable for us to

9. These words were spoken at the inaugural address of the Free University of Amsterdam in 1880. See James D. Bratt, ed., *Abraham Kuyper: A Centennial Reader* (Grand Rapids: Eerdmans, 1998), 461.

behold God as He appears in His only begotten Son than to investigate His secret essence.[10]

This sounds a note entirely and persistently characteristic of Calvin. His words afford us the broad theological perspective from which we may best approach his specific teaching on union with Christ.

THE PRINCIPLE OF FAITH

Although some Calvin scholars have argued that it has received a disproportionate amount of attention in accounts of his thought, Calvin's *Institutes of the Christian Religion* remains a compendium of Christian doctrine which he revised several times over the years and provides a good summary account of his teaching.[11] In his introduction to the 1560 French edition, Calvin declared that he thought of his work as 'a key to open a way for all children of God into a good and right understanding of Holy Scripture'.[12] It was written in four books. The first dealt with the knowledge of God, the Creator; the second with the knowledge of God, our Redeemer in Christ; the third with the way in which we receive the grace of Christ; and the final one with the Church. Union with Christ is treated in the third book and the following account will concentrate on the exposition of this subject as he provides it in this book. In doing so, we

---

10. Calvin, *Commentaries on the Second Epistle of Paul to the Corinthians and the Epistles to Timothy, Titus and Philemon* (Edinburgh: St Andrew Press, 1964), 57–8.

11. Alister E. McGrath is justified in proceeding in this way in *A Life of John Calvin* (Oxford: Blackwell, 1990), 145–7.

12. *Institutes*, I.vii.

shall, arguably, be treating the heart of Calvin's theology.[13] In the second book, Calvin had described how God has reconciled us to himself through Jesus Christ. However, he tells us at the beginning of Book 3 that this will be of no profit to us unless we are joined to Christ by 'the secret energy of the Spirit'. Indeed, 'as long as Christ remains outside of us, and we are separated from him, all that he has suffered and done for the salvation of the human race remains useless and of no value for us' (i.1). In Christ we find all that God has for us: 'until our minds become intent upon the Spirit, Christ, so to speak, lies idle because we coldly contemplate him as outside ourselves' (i.3). The third book is thus fundamentally about the Spirit, who joins us to Christ. On its surface it may appear to be more about faith than about the Spirit, but the reason for that appearance is that the chief work of the Spirit is that of producing faith in us, that faith by which we are joined to Christ.

What, then, is the nature of faith? Calvin regards two interpretations as inadequate. Firstly, faith is not rightly understood as mere assent to the truth of Christian doctrine or of the history narrated in Scripture. Obviously, Calvin does not doubt that such assent is important. Someone who fought so hard to promote the doctrinal tenets of Reformed Protestantism and who held such a high view of Scripture, elaborated in the first book of the Institutes, could hardly think otherwise. But what does 'assent' amount to? It amounts to an intellectual agreement, a mental concurrence. It is possible, however, to embrace mentally the truth of Christian doctrine

---

13. This is argued by Charles Partee in a comprehensive recent introduction to *The Theology of John Calvin* (Louisville: Westminster John Knox, 2008). From now on, references to Calvin's *Institutes* will be incorporated, as often as possible, into the body of the text.

and accept unreservedly the history narrated in Scripture without possessing that faith which is generated by the secret energy of the Spirit. Believing that something is the case may be important; but that kind of believing is not what Scripture means by 'faith'. Sometimes, in the history of theology, a distinction has been drawn between fides historica and fides salvifica ('historical faith' and 'saving faith') – faith as assent and faith as saving trust. This distinction captures much of what Calvin picks out in the Institutes when he denies the adequacy of what some people mean by 'faith'.

Secondly, faith is more than simply knowledge of God's will towards us, as declared in the Bible. Granted, this view of faith is richer, fuller, more intimate and more personal than the first. Someone who says, 'I know how God is disposed towards us' has gone further along the path of faith than someone who merely says 'I believe Christian doctrine' or 'I believe that Scripture rightly records the story of salvation.' For the question of our relationship with God has now come into view. And, of course, Calvin does not doubt that knowing how God is disposed towards us is an important facet of faith. As it stands, however, this knowledge still does not take us far enough. We are still one step removed from what Calvin understands as biblical faith. We remain on the level of the general and theological; transformation of existence is not yet indicated. This faith remains within the orbit of assent rather than expressing the heart of vital faith. While Calvin was keen to emphasise the distinction between knowing God in his essence (which is impossible) and knowing how God is disposed towards us (which is important), the latter yet remains insufficient if we wish to possess full-orbed biblical faith.

How, then, are we to understand faith? 'We shall possess a right definition of faith if we call it a firm and certain knowledge of God's benevolence toward us, founded upon the truth of the freely given promise in Christ, both revealed to our minds and sealed upon our hearts through the Holy Spirit' (ii.7). Again:

> Here is the chief hinge on which faith turns: that we do not regard the promises of mercy that God offers as true only outside ourselves, but not at all in us; rather that we make them ours by inwardly embracing them (ii.16).

Inward assurance is the heart of faith. What we are assured of lies outside us, in the form of the person and work of Jesus Christ on the cross. But assurance itself is obviously an inward matter. It is more than a union of mind with the truth by intellectual conviction. It is a vital union of the soul with its redeemer, an 'embracing' of the divine promises which is an embracing of Christ. From the believer's point of view, we embrace Christ; from the divine point of view, the Spirit 'seals' on our hearts the promises. This, in sum, is the connection between the subject of faith and the subject of union with Christ: faith is the primary work of the Spirit and this faith constitutes a living union and not a mere assent or mental conviction.

Calvin's way of understanding faith here is easily misunderstood. If conviction and assurance are regarded by him as important, is this a case of being presumptuous? Had Calvin stopped at his second definition, one he finds inadequate, we might not find ourselves making the query, for there is surely nothing presumptuous or arrogant in believing that God is generally well disposed in Christ towards humanity. No presumption is involved because we are simply believing his word. But to say that God is gracious to *me* in particular and that, in embracing Christ, *I* may be sure of how God regards *me* seems to take matters a step further. Would it not be more suitable to the nature of faith not to presume too much; to venture forth in life with a degree of confidence, but not a full measure of it; to await the outcome of a life lived, not to anticipate a destiny, which we seem to be doing if we embrace for *ourselves* a *promise* of salvation based on the work of Christ and the Spirit, believed and experienced in the present?

At least two observations are in order to explain Calvin's position in response to this challenge. Firstly, when we think of it, would I be consistent if I were intellectually convinced that God had a good will towards humanity in general but was not inwardly convinced that he was benevolently disposed towards me in particular? What would be the point, force and effect of the disclosure of a divine general disposition towards the generality of humankind if we could not apply it with confidence to ourselves in particular? Secondly, in Calvin's theology, we are speaking of the work of the Spirit in producing assurance, not of humans working themselves up psychologically to a pitch of religious certainty. The Spirit, like the wind, 'blows where it pleases' (Jn 3:8); it is the Spirit's prerogative to apply the benefits of the work of Christ to the believer and invest his or her heart with corresponding assurance. Presumption would kick in if we *denied* that this was desirable and possible for God, not if we *affirm* it.

There is an essential background to all this which we must take into account if we want to understand both what Calvin is saying and why he says it. It concerns the matter of assurance of our standing before God. It is misleading to speak of 'the' Protestant Reformation as though it were a single one. There were Protestant Reformations which took diverse forms and were rooted in different lands and contexts.[14] When people speak of 'Reformation' origins, special attention is normally accorded to Martin Luther in Germany, and the spiritual struggle which lay behind the impetus to reformation is familiarly described in terms of Luther's question: 'How may I find a gracious God?' It is a quest for assurance. The presupposition of the quest is that the human conscience is burdened by failure and that obedience to the law of God does not suffice to secure acceptance before God because our sin is far too strong for us to be victorious and our guilt too well-grounded for our consciences to be genuinely pacified. 'Genuinely' is an important word here, for there were devices for the pacification of conscience which the Church of his day promoted and Luther's resistance to this joined to his proclamation of the alternative – that justification is by faith alone – formed the theological backbone of the German and Lutheran Reformation. This is not true of the German Reformation alone: we find in Calvin a similar emphasis.[15] The human predicament lies in the fact that we are justly condemned for our sin but are unable to remove the weight of condemnation by our efforts. In mercy, God delivers us through Jesus Christ, but the benefits of Christ are apprehended by faith alone. Neither Luther nor Calvin thought for one moment that this made the life of faith indifferent to obedient works. On the contrary, both emphasised strongly that faith is the root and spring of

14. A solid textbook and introduction by Carter Lindberg is titled *The European Reformations* (Chichester: Wiley-Blackwell, 2010), the plurality extending to Protestantisms. Although it is true that Protestantisms have fragmented, we should always remember that 'Protestantism' did not start historically as a single entity.

15. In his *Institutes*, Calvin remarks that justification is 'the main hinge on which religion turns' (III.ii.1).

vital life-transformation. But assurance of our standing before God, the assurance that he has accepted us in Christ, can not be purchased by our works. Faith alone lays hold of reconciliation and the assurance that is meant to accompany it.

An assurance of our standing before God is important because, without it, the conscience is burdened and God designs to bestow upon us a tranquil conscience, not so that we subsequently become heedless and presumptuous, but precisely because it frees our energies for the service of God. For Calvin, then, the fact that union with Christ should bear fruit in assurance was no small matter. Faith is meant to be confident. At the same time, Calvin recognised that it was not as simple as that: faith operates in the arena of struggle and assurance is neither easy nor automatic. The second chapter of Book 3 of the *Institutes* is the second longest we have yet encountered in Calvin's work and in it he tries to view faith from a number of angles – its assurance and struggle, its confidence and striving. If we ask why it was important for him that faith should embrace assurance, apart from the reasons already given for this, we should have to say that he held that we honour God by being assured of the reliable truth of his promises towards us. Proper assurance, then, stems from trust, not from presumption.

We may have given the impression so far that Calvin is individualistic, focused on the inwardness, assurance, faith and conscience of the individual, so that the notion of union with Christ is, correspondingly, highly personal. This is a half-truth. It is true to the extent that Calvin was profoundly conscious of the fact that, as Paul put it, 'we must all appear before the judgement seat of Christ, that each one may receive what is due to him for the things done while in the body, whether good or bad' (2 Cor 5:10). 'Though this is something that applies to all men,' Calvin comments, 'all men do not have minds sufficiently exalted to remember every single moment that they must appear before the judgement-seat of Christ.'[16] We can not, by sheltering in any institution or appealing to the corporate nature of faith and the Church, avoid the individualism of God's eschatological judgement. Calvin combines with this a strong ecclesiology. We shall later note the ecclesial aspect of the way that he understands union with Christ when we turn to what he says about the Eucharist. Here, we merely recall the fact that, sometimes, Protestant individualism is criticised by recalling Cyprian's description of the Church as our 'mother', without whom or which we can not truly have God as Father. What comes as a surprise to many is that Calvin not only affirms that the Church is our mother, but actually underlines it by opening his exposition of the doctrine of the Church in Book 4 of the *Institutes* by underlining the fact.[17] The charge of individualist distortion of ecclesiology may apply to forms of Protestantism, but an investigation of Calvin in this respect encourages a rather different judgement.

THE LIFE OF FAITH

What, then, is the shape of the life of faith? We may pick out at least three characteristics of the life of faith, the life which is lived in union with Jesus Christ.

---

16. *Commentaries on Second Corinthians*, 71. This is one of those passages in his commentaries where Calvin briefly explains the consistency of being judged by works and being justified by faith, but refers his readers to the *Institutes* for fuller discussion.

17. *Institutes* IV.iv.1–4. The editor of the translation of the *Institutes* which I have been using explicitly cites Cyprian at this point (1016, n. 10). However, I do not mean to affirm that Catholic and Calvinist derive from this description the same theological conclusions.

Firstly, it is a life brimful of good works. Calvin speaks of holiness as the bond of our 'union with God' which is a strong, but consistent, way of referring to our union with Christ. 'We are consecrated and dedicated to God in order that we may thereafter think, speak, meditate, and do, nothing except to his glory' (III.vii.1). Secondly, it is a life of self-denial, endurance and suffering – in short, a life of bearing the cross: 'consulting our self-interest is the pestilence that most effectively leads to our destruction' (vii.1). Why so? Because 'whomever the Lord has adopted and deemed worthy of his fellowship ought to prepare themselves for a hard, toilsome, unquiet life, crammed with very many and various kinds of evil' (III.viii.1). Our self-dedication must be complete: 'he alone has duly denied himself who has so totally resigned himself to the Lord that he permits every part of his life to be governed by God's will'. (vii.10) Thirdly, it is a life of rejoicing in the good things of life, the necessary and the delightful alike, whether food or wine, trees or flowers, smells or colours. Calvin asks:

> Did [God] not endow gold and silver, ivory and marble, with a loveliness that renders them more precious than other metals or stones? Did he not, in short render many things attractive to us, apart from their necessary use? (10.2).

Obedience, self-denial and joy – all these must take their proper form in us when they are rooted in the soil of prayer. In fact, prayer 'is the chief exercise of faith'.[18] Effective prayer requires at least four things: firstly, concentration on God; secondly, a sincere and penitent acknowledgement of our need; thirdly, the

---

18. So Calvin titles this chapter of the third book (iii.20) which opens volume 2 of the *Institutes* in the translation from which I am quoting.

renunciation of confidence in ourselves with an accompanying plea for pardon; fourthly, confident hope in God. Prayer does not come easily. 'To pray rightly is a rare gift' (III.xx.5), for 'no heart can ever break into sincere calling upon God that does not at the same time aspire to godliness' (xx.10). Calvin steers his exposition here by the light of the summons to repentance and faith which so explicitly marks the presentation of the gospel as recorded for us by the Synoptic evangelists. For 'it is faith that obtains whatever is granted to prayer' (xx.11) and 'lawful prayer ... demands repentance' (xx.7).

It was indicated earlier that, in outlining Calvin's understanding of life in union with Christ, we were doing little more than following the main line of his exposition in Book 3 of the *Institutes*. In the course of this, we noted that Calvin had a robust ecclesiology and in the course of his ecclesiology we encounter a sorely neglected aspect of Calvin's thought which, as a matter of fact, lies right at the heart of his thinking about union with Christ. This is his teaching on the Eucharist or the Lord's Supper. It comes as a considerable surprise to many to discover what Calvin believed on this subject. Have standard Presbyterian theological assumptions and ecclesial practice departed further from Calvin's theology than at this point? Possibly only in the neglect of his social teaching.[19] The broad ecumenical context of our present enquiry into Calvin's understanding of union with Christ impels us to pause at this point to secure the basics of his theology.

---

19. In practice, churches belonging to the Reformed tradition may have departed a long way from Calvin on, for example, justification or predestination, but there may be a vague awareness of or sense of familiarity with his position on these issues when it is presented to those churches, whereas his teaching on the Eucharist and the centrality of social reformation come as a complete surprise.

Differences over sacramental theology seem to lie at the very heart of the historic disagreements between Catholicism and Protestantism. But this is an area where Protestants have never been united. No intra-Protestant theological dispute in the sixteenth century was more bitter than that over the sacraments, the Eucharist in particular, and division between Luther and Zwingli was deep on this question. Calvin expended considerable energy in trying to bring into closer accord on this question the varieties of Continental Protestantism. Perhaps he was attempting to square the circle. Speaking generally, Protestants have been united in differing from Catholics on two matters here, rejecting both transubstantiation and the Mass as a sacrifice. But if it is relatively clear what Protestants have rejected, what have they positively believed? This is where the differences surface. In contrast to Lutheran belief that the body of Christ was inexplicably present with, in and under the species of bread and wine, the position taken by the Swiss Reformation traditions is usually described as a form of memorialism. That is, the Lord's Supper is a remembrance that Jesus Christ died for us. Christ is not really present in the bread and wine. All thought of sacramental union with Christ seems to be out of the question.

As a matter of fact, Zwingli's own position was by no means as crude as this.[20] But, in any case, he is not our quarry. If Zwingli is less extreme, from a Catholic or a Lutheran point of view, than is usually believed, Calvin is closer still than Zwingli, although

---

20. See W.P. Stephens, *The Theology of Huldrych Zwingli* (Oxford: Clarendon, 1986), chapter 11. Stephens refers to, without endorsing, Locher's judgement that Zwingli interpreted 'memorial' or 'remembrance' in a way typical of the Platonised student of Augustine that he was, i.e., in terms of the realisation of presence and not of retrospection (245).

there is room to argue about precisely where Calvin's position should be plotted in relation to both Luther and Zwingli. Calvin (and at this particular point he is close to Zwingli) thought that when we conceive of the presence of Christ in the world, we must conceive of his humanity as being present in heaven. In adumbrating his position, he was participating in a Christological discussion that had occupied theologians of the undivided Church in the patristic and medieval periods who subscribed to the belief that Jesus Christ, the Son of God, is one person possessing both a divine and a human nature. The Christological consensus of the Church was roughly that, according to his eternal reality, the Son, or Word, of God was omnipresent in the world but, when he took on human flesh, he assumed a genuine humanity, a humanity circumscribed within a particular space and time. How God the Son could be ubiquitous in his divine nature but localised in his human nature was a mystery, yet there was nothing unreasonable in maintaining such a belief, for why should a God of power be incapable of creating a world in which he could become incarnate? The way of incarnation is a mystery, but the fact of it is intelligible. Calvin, along with the Catholic Church, was heir to this patristic tradition. When Calvin conceived of Jesus Christ as being present in heaven, his conception was centred on the risen *humanity* of Jesus Christ, the one who had been truly enfleshed in our world and who remained human, albeit in a mode transcending our comprehension, to all eternity, without ceasing to be divine.[21]

---

21. For the ontological questions surrounding this, see T.F. Torrance, *Space, Time and Incarnation* (London, New York & Toronto: Oxford University Press, 1969).

As Calvin saw it, the bread and the wine could not become the body and blood of Christ.[22] For the bread and wine are here below and the risen humanity of Christ is above. What does *not* follow from this, however, is that, in the Eucharist, we only *remember* the death of Jesus Christ on our behalf. What Calvin emphasises is that, in eucharistic communion, the Spirit which gives us life raises us heavenward to where Jesus Christ is seated, there to feed on him by faith. Christ's is a real presence of the most definite and concrete kind – not the real presence of the human flesh and blood Jesus Christ transubstantiated in the bread and wine itself, but the real presence of the heavenly Christ with whom the believing participant in the sacrament has real communion.

It is doubtful if Calvin anywhere in the *Institutes* alludes to 'mystery' as much as he does in the chapter where he expounds this position. In sum:

> Whenever this matter is discussed, when I have tried to say all, I feel that I have as yet said little in proportion to its worth. And although my mind can think beyond what my tongue can utter, yet even my mind is conquered and overwhelmed by the greatness of the thing. Therefore, nothing remains but to break forth in wonder at this mystery, which plainly neither the mind is able to conceive nor the tongue to express (IV.xvii.7).

Biographical and theological accounts of Calvin may convey conflicting impressions as to whether he wanted to celebrate the Lord's Supper monthly or weekly. In establishing his position, we have to take into account a range of data including both

---

22. I make no assumptions here about how the position of the Catholic Church on transubstantiation should be theologically described.

Calvin's theological pronouncements and what was practically possible or desirable at a given time in Geneva. However, from the *Institutes* we learn that the Lord's Supper can hardly be partaken of too frequently (IV.xvii.43–44).

Conclusion

In the foregoing account, I have aimed neither to advocate nor to distance myself from Calvin's theology, simply to try to understand and give an account of it. Much has been omitted, but it is hoped that the main lines of his way of thinking about living in union with Christ have been fairly presented. Whatever our judgements on Calvin and whatever else we find in him apart from those things to which we have attended, it is surely not unduly partisan to say confidently that there is a theological richness in his contribution and a vital sense of life in union with Christ which has the capacity to nourish the soul of the believing individual and the Church of Jesus Christ in our day. Union with Jesus Christ is something whose outworking must be expressed in all the detail of social, political, economic and cultural life. Time and eternity, history and eschatology are united in this outlook as surely as Christ is joined to the church and to the believer. To begin to acquaint ourselves with Calvin's perspective on union with Christ is probably as good a way as any to begin to acquaint ourselves with Calvin's theology.

CHAPTER 2

Ignatius of Loyola (1491–1556): Christian Soldier or 'Soul-aider'?

Salvador Ryan

In 1528, two giants of Reformation Europe may well have passed each other in the streets of Paris where both were students at the Collège de Montaigu. John Calvin was leaving the university when Ignatius of Loyola, his senior by some eighteen years, was just arriving. What follows is a short introduction to the life of the second of these towering figures of the sixteenth century.

FORMATIVE INFLUENCES

The future founder of the Jesuit order was born an *hidalgo* (*hijo de algo* in its longer form, means literally a 'son of something' or as might be more colloquially put, 'a somebody'), that is the son of a member of the Spanish minor nobility. He was born in 1491 and grew up at the castle of Loyola in the Basque country in the far north-east of Castile. Although his birth name was Iñigo Lopez Recalde de Oñaz y de Loyola, he would become known to history simply as Ignatius, for when he was later at the Collège Saint Barbe in Paris he began to refer to himself not as Iñigo but as Ignacio, which he believed was a variant of his birth name.[1]

---

1. John W. O'Malley, *The First Jesuits* (Cambridge, Mass: Harvard University Press, 1993), 29.

When he matriculated from the University of Paris, this would be the name which would be recorded for him.

The year of Ignatius's birth (1491) was a significant one in the history of Spain. The centuries-long process of *reconquista* ('reconquering') of Spain from the Moors, who had dominated much of the Iberian peninsula since the eighth century, was about to be achieved. The following year (1492), the last Islamic kingdom of Granada in the far south would fall into Christian hands. In this, Spain proved to be a remarkable exception to the rule in the history of crusading Europe and could boast of extirpating an Islamic power on Iberian soil in a rare reversal of Muslim advance. It must be remembered, that in a very real sense, there did not yet exist a political entity that can truly be called 'Spain'. The peninsula was comprised of a number of political entities with their own languages, among them the kingdom of Castile, the Crown of Aragon (which comprised the kingdom of Aragon, the kingdom of Valencia and the county of Barcelona or Catalonia), the kingdom of Navarre, the kingdom of Portugal and the Muslim kingdom of Granada. These kingdoms would retain a great deal of independence long after the union of Aragon and Castile through the marriage of Ferdinand V of Aragón and Isabella of Castile in 1469.

The centuries-long struggle against the cultures of Judaism and Islam which characterised much of Spanish Catholicism's history ensured that its variety of Catholicism was particularly militant. In the fourteenth and fifteenth centuries many Jews and Muslims in Spain had thought it prudent to convert to Christianity. These new Christian converts (convert Jews were known as *Conversos* and Muslims as *Moriscos*) were never fully trusted by their 'old Christian' counterparts and their loyalty to the joint monarchy of Ferdinand and Isabella was often held in doubt. Such tensions were particularly evident in late fifteenth-century Castile when Ignatius grew up. In the early 1480s, a new version of the Inquisition under direct royal control was introduced to Castile by the joint monarchy (the Inquisition had never been allowed to operate there before). Its aim was to root out Judaisers (converted Jews who were thought to be still practising their Jewish rituals in secret) and between 1481 and 1488 it would burn some 700 suspects alive. When the Moorish stronghold of Granada fell in 1492, Queen Isabella gave all her Jewish subjects in Castile the choice to convert to Christianity within three months or to face exile from Spain.[2]

Within Spanish Catholicism itself, the late fifteenth century saw the occurrence of something akin to a 'Reformation before the Reformation', which was promoted by a Spanish monarchy eager to stamp out structural abuses and to keep Spanish Christianity free of heresy. The chief ecclesiastical figure behind this movement was a Castilian Observant Franciscan, Francisco Ximénes de Cisneros (1436–1517) who was appointed confessor to Queen Isabella in 1494 and Archbishop of Toledo in the following year.[3] In significant ways, Ximénes' reforms would anticipate those which would later be legislated for universally at the Council of Trent. He called for a closer observance of the Rule of St Francis and apostolic poverty among some of the more relaxed Franciscan friaries. He also required the friars and members of other religious orders, as well as the secular clergy, to put aside some lax ways of life to which they had become accustomed. These requirements included giving up the practice of having wives or concubines, of living in the

---

2. Diarmaid MacCulloch, *Reformation: Europe's House Divided, 1490–1700* (London: Allen Lane, 2003), 58–60.

3. Michael Walsh, *The Cardinals* (Norwich: Canterbury Press, 2010), 155.

parishes in which they were supposed to be based and attending to the administration of the sacraments: hardly unreasonable, it must be said! Not all religious, however, were willing to be reformed: by the end of the century some three hundred friars had fled to Morocco with their wives and concubines where many of them would convert to Islam.[4] Ximénes also founded the University of Alcalá and funded the printing of a huge number of books on his favourite mystical authors so that they could be made available to the literate public. One of his most impressive projects was the funding of the Complutensian Polyglot Bible, the first printed polyglot of the entire Bible. In 1507 he would be made a cardinal, the same year as he took up the post of Inquisitor General during which time he had thousands of non-Christian manuscripts and books burned.[5] Many of those within monasteries and friaries who wished to promote spiritual reform and to renew the Church came from the circles of the *conversos* and, because of their associations with Judaism, were regarded with some suspicion. The rise of prominent Jewish *conversos* through the ranks of the nobility and the Church had been going on for over a century since the violent pogroms of 1391. One of the most remarkable examples is that of the learned Rabbi of Burgos, Selomah ha-Levi, who converted to Christianity in 1390, studied theology in Paris and became a bishop (changing his name to Pablo de Santa María), a position which would also be held by many of the children

---

4. Walsh, *The Cardinals*, 155; for the reform of monastic spirituality see especially Terence O'Reilly, 'Meditation and contemplation: monastic spirituality in early sixteenth-century Spain', in Lesley Twomey, ed., *Faith and Fanaticism: Religious Fervour in Early Modern Spain* (Aldershot: Ashgate, 1997), 37–57.

5. MacCulloch, *Reformation*, 61.

fathered before his episcopacy and other relatives.[6] Prominent *converso* prelates would do much to sow seeds of renewal within Spanish Catholicism and by 1500 these had produced a movement of mystical and spiritual enthusiasm which became known as *alumbradismo,* or 'illuminism', and its practitioners *alumbrados* ('enlightened ones').

These *alumbrados,* the Spanish Inquisition found, drew their inspiration from reading sections of the Bible available in Spanish and also northern European spiritual works associated with what was known as the *Devotio Moderna,* the most famous of which was *The Imitation of Christ* of Thomas à Kempis. Mystics who were seen to go too far, who 'abandoned themselves' to the love of God (*dexados*), were viewed as dangerous by the Inquisition and were to be rooted out.[7] Some *alumbrados* would later take an interest in some of the spiritual writings of a young Augustinian monk from Erfurt, Martin Luther, and this did little to help their case with the Spanish ecclesiastical authorities who condemned the movement of *alumbradismo* in 1525.[8]

This, then, was the Spain into which Ignatius was born: a Spain with a long tradition of Christian crusading and even the staging of mock battles between *cristianos y moros* so that Christianity's triumph over the Moors would not be forgotten even after their expulsion from Granada in 1492. Although traditionally best known as a soldier, Ignatius's first ambition was, in fact, to advance at the Castilian court, and his training in

---

6. Teófilo F. Ruiz, *Spain's Centuries of Crisis, 1300–1474* (Oxford: Wiley-Blackwell, 2007), 159.

7. MacCulloch, *Reformation,* 64–5.

8. For a comprehensive account of illuminism, see Alastair Hamilton, *Heresy and Mysticism in Sixteenth-Century Spain: The Alumbrados* (Toronto: University of Toronto Press, 1992).

skilfully negotiating social niceties among the powerful would stand him in good stead later on.[9] Part and parcel of his career path was always going to include military service and it would be necessary to adopt the posturing of medieval chivalry if he were to advance as an Iberian courtier. When he was about thirteen he was sent by his father to the household of the chief treasurer to King Ferdinand of Aragón at Arévalo where he was trained in the manners expected of a courtier.[10] Arévalo was important for other reasons too. It was the centre of the Spanish Franciscan renewal promoted by Cardinal Ximenez. Three years later (1517) Ignatius entered military service. In 1521, King Francis I of France began the first phase of a protracted series of wars with the newly elected Holy Roman Emperor, Charles V Habsburg (1519) who had also been King of Spain since 1516. It was during the course of an ultimately futile defence of the citadel at Pamplona against the French that Ignatius was to receive serious injuries (his right leg smashed by a cannon ball and his left also badly wounded) and which led to his return home to the castle of Loyola to convalesce.

The Journey of Conversion

In recovering from the injured leg which had been badly set by a doctor of the victorious French army, the books that were available for Ignatius to read were not the chivalric romances he would have preferred but, instead, a fourteenth-century *Life of Christ* by Ludolf of Saxony (d. 1378) and a Castilian translation of the thirteenth-century bestseller, the *Legenda Aurea* or 'Golden Legend', a collection of fantastic tales of the deeds and often

---

9. MacCulloch, *Reformation*, 220.

10. Jonathan Wright, *The Jesuits: Missions, Myths and Histories* (London: Harper Perennial, 2005), 16.

gruesome martyrdoms of the Christian saints. Here, Loyola encountered a Christianised chivalry presented through the great saints as knights of God. As he read, he found that when he contemplated the imitation of figures such as Dominic and Francis he was left with a sense of peace and comfort, while any inclination to continue in his former life left him dry and agitated.[11] In this he believed that God was speaking to him through his experience. While reading these works, he studied them closely in order to eke out their deepest meaning, reading them again and again and making notes. This, for Ignatius, was the beginning of a dramatic process of conversion which would culminate at the pilgrimage site of Montserrat near Barcelona and the hermitage of Manresa.

In his spiritual autobiography (1553–1555),[12] Loyola would regard this experience after the battle of Pamplona as dividing his life into what Michael Mullett calls 'two sharply contrasted moral panels': the first given over to the vanities of the world and the second to an awakening of a new life of faith.[13] Despite describing his pre-conversion life as an *hidalgo* as one in which he was free with women and carnal desires, Ignatius remained circumspect in his description of his supposed vices, leading some commentators to wonder whether his life had, in fact, been as licentious as he wished to portray it: the greater the sin, the more impressive the conversion, so to speak. We do know, however, that as a fifteen-year-old on a visit home to Loyola he was cited in court for brawling, but he pleaded that he had been

---

11. O'Malley, *The First Jesuits*, 24.

12. An English translation is available, *The Autobiography of St Ignatius Loyola, with Related Documents*, ed. John Olin (New York: Fordham University Press, 1992).

13. Michael A. Mullett, *The Catholic Reformation* (London and New York: Routledge, 1999), 76.

tonsured and therefore enjoyed clerical status, this being a legal convenience in getting himself off the hook.[14]

We should be wary of regarding Ignatius's experience of convalescence and his discovery of spiritual reading as something hitherto wholly alien to him. It would be simplistic to assume that, on his convalescent bed, Ignatius was simply a *tabula rasa* on which these late-medieval devotional works impressed themselves by sheer chance. It might rather be argued that Ignatius was far more rooted in late-medieval piety than is often allowed. Loyola's family themselves were so coloured by that piety, that they actually had available on their bookshelves Castilian translations of these devotional works. As has already been seen, he served as a court page at Arévalo, the centre of the Spanish Franciscan renewal promoted by Cardinal Ximenez. Ignatius's encounter with these writings may well have been that of a mind whose soil had been well prepared in advance. Ludolf of Saxony's work was hardly a kind of late-medieval equivalent of *Mysticism for Dummies*: it was rather a demanding treatise of Carthusian spirituality.

Eager to imitate the lives and heroism of the saints, Ignatius resolved to go to Jerusalem as a pilgrim and, while there, to set about converting the Muslims. This would be the ultimate quest of Christian chivalry. Before embarking upon his trip to Jerusalem, he would, in keeping with the classic knightly style, keep a 'vigil of arms' before the pilgrimage statue of the Black Madonna at Montserrat in Catalonia (25 March 1522). There he dedicated himself as a knight about to depart for Jerusalem by setting down his sword and dagger and taking up a pilgrim's staff and the clothing of a beggar. From now on

---

14. O'Malley, *The First Jesuits*, 23.

he would clothe himself 'with the armour of Christ'.[15] At the reformed Benedictine monastery of Montserrat, he followed a modified version of the practice of the Benedictine novices before investiture by taking three days to write down all his sins up to that point before making a general confession.

Ignatius would express his encounter with God in terms which he knew best: the chivalric expression of duty and service. His Marian devotion was similarly formed as he devoted himself to the service of a certain lady: Mary. When setting off on his planned pilgrimage to Jerusalem in 1523, he got into conversation with a Muslim who ill-advisedly voiced doubts about Mary's virginity, whereupon Loyola considered murdering the man 'to avenge [Mary's] honour'.[16] His continued attachment to the ideals of chivalry may well have been reinforced by Ludolf of Saxony's use of the image of Christ as a chivalric knight, yet he would swap his original role models, such as Roland and Oliver, for Francis and Dominic whom he hoped to emulate in ambitious spiritual feats.

Leaving Montserrat, Ignatius travelled to the small town of Manresa, planning to spend only a few days there, but due to an outbreak of plague his visit was extended to almost a year. There he went through a particularly ascetical phase, adopting a discipline reminiscent of the desert fathers of early monasticism including prayer, fasting and self-flagellation. He also allowed his hair, fingernails and toenails to grow longer and longer and abandoned all care for his body, as a reaction against the preening which he had formerly devoted to his appearance.[17]

---

15. Carter Lindberg, *The European Reformations* (2nd ed., Oxford: Wiley-Blackwell, 2009), 334.

16. Mullett, *The Catholic Reformation*, 78.

17. O'Malley, *The First Jesuits*, 25.

He would recall later how, at that time, he reckoned that 'holiness was entirely measured by exterior austerity of life and that he who did the most austere penances would be held in the divine estimation for the most holy ...' At this point he wished to make satisfaction for his sins by extreme austerity. Later, with the benefit of spiritual maturity, he would caution his fellow Jesuits against the kind of self-starvation he imposed upon himself 'eating nothing but herbs': 'if the Jesuit sees that a certain degree of abstinence means that he has neither the bodily strength nor the moderation for his spiritual exercises, he will easily come to estimate what is the right amount to keep up his physical strength ...'[18]

Beginning in March 1522 at Manresa, Ignatius would experience a series of extraordinarily intense visionary experiences which involved seeing the Virgin and Child and, more ominously, wayside crosses turning into diabolical shapes.[19] These would not help Ignatius's reputation of religious orthodoxy in a Spain which was nervous about such events, given especially its recent problems with the *alumbrado,* or illuminist, heresy which was thought to claim direct inspiration independent of the Church and Scripture. Ignatius later described one of those moments of enlightenment as being so powerful that he would have believed what it contained 'even if there were no scriptures' that taught the same thing.[20] This idea of Ignatius being directly 'taught by God' greatly concerned the authorities and Ignatius soon attracted the attention of the Spanish Inquisition.

---

18. Mullett, *The Catholic Reformation*, 78–9.

19. Ibid., 79.

20. O'Malley, *The First Jesuits*, 25.

At Manresa, Ignatius would also undergo bouts of deep depression with a heightened anxiety over the possibility of damnation and even temptations towards suicide. Like Luther, he also experienced acute scruples over whether he could, in fact, achieve true and perfect contrition for his sins. In addition, he embarked upon a hunger strike of sorts which he intended to continue until God took care of him. After a week of self-imposed starvation, however, his confessor ordered him to break his fast, an order which he disobeyed.[21] The Manresa experience had driven Ignatius close to the edge and it was only being welcomed into the routine of the monastic office and the companionship of the Benedictines at Montserrat which put him on the road to recovery, and restored him to a more balanced way of living. Yet the psychological and spiritual crisis which he experienced at Manresa might also be read as part and parcel of his conversion process which had begun on his sickbed at Loyola. The Jesuit scholar W.W. Meissner has examined these experiences in some depth from a psychoanalytical perspective.[22] On the instruction of his Benedictine confessor, Ignatius would jot down his changing spiritual experiences. These would become the raw material for his systematically organised guide to prayer, self-examination and surrender, which would eventually reach print in a papally approved format in 1548 as the *Spiritual Exercises*.[23]

A MISSION UNDER SUSPICION

Early in 1523 Ignatius finally set off for Jerusalem, taking the route from Barcelona to Genoa and on through Rome, then

---

21. Mullett, *The Catholic Reformation*, 80.

22. W.W. Meissner, *Ignatius of Loyola: the Psychology of a Saint* (New Haven: Yale University Press, 1994).

23. MacCulloch, *Reformation*, 221.

Venice and Cyprus. On his sea voyages he limited his food intake to ships' biscuits. He did not always ingratiate himself with the sailors on board, often rashly chastising them for their habit of cursing, and his unappreciated interjections nearly saw him marooned.[24] In setting off to the Holy Land, he wanted to imitate Francis of Assisi and spend his time as a pilgrim in the city. Ignatius arrived there in the autumn of 1523 and spent a fortnight visiting the holy sites. He initially wanted to live out the rest of his days there, but the local Franciscans, acutely aware of the complicated relations that existed with their Turkish overlords, requested him to leave. He was reluctant to do so at first until the Franciscans eventually threatened him with excommunication if he did not comply.[25]

On his return to Europe, Ignatius may have already been contemplating entering religious life. Realising that he had no Latin, he spent the years from 1524–1526 learning the language at a grammar school in Barcelona, in the company of children many years his junior.[26] To support himself he begged for food. From there, he moved with his newly acquired faltering Latin, to the University at Alcalá where, for some months, he set about studying scholastic theology. He continued to study sporadically, supporting himself by begging. He also began to guide people through the *Spiritual Exercises*, taught catechism and was a weekly communicant (an unusual practice for the time). It should be noted that Alcalá was renowned in 1526 as a centre of Erasmian humanism.

---

24. Mullett, *The Catholic Reformation*, 82.

25. O'Malley, *The First Jesuits*, 25–6.

26. Mullett, *The Catholic Reformation*, 83.

It was at Alcalá that he came to the attention of the Spanish Inquisition of Toledo as a possible *alumbrado* and was imprisoned for forty-two days at one stage.[27] Just a year earlier, the Inquisitor General had issued an edict of faith attributed to the *alumbrados* which consisted of some forty-eight so-called propositions of the movement which included contempt for the cult of the saints, the veneration of images, papal bulls, indulgences, fasting and the commandments of the Church; the edict also claimed that *alumbrados* practised passive reliance on the divine will, which was thought to bring about perfection. The edict was directed against those who 'call themselves enlightened, abandoned and perfect'.[28] When Ignatius arrived in Alcalá he had certainly become acquainted with some *alumbrados* including the Portuguese priest called Manuel de Miona, whom he chose for his confessor (and who would later become a Jesuit himself). It is understandable that the Inquisition concluded that Ignatius himself subscribed to these tenets. Because he gave special attention to observing Saturday as a special day in honour of Mary, Ignatius was interrogated by the Inquisition on suspicion that he might be observing a form of the Jewish Sabbath.[29] The fact that he continued to wear the garb of a pilgrim rather than that of a student did not help matters much either (he and his 'sack-wearing' friends were suspected of being *alumbrados*). On being found innocent, he was instructed to dress like other students and not to speak in public about religion until he had pursued his course of studies.[30]

---

27. O'Malley, *The First Jesuits*, 27.

28. Brian O'Leary, 'The mysticism of Ignatius of Loyola', *Review of Ignatian Spirituality* 38:3 (2007), 85.

29. Mullett, *The Catholic Reformation*, 84.

30. O'Malley, *The First Jesuits*, 27.

What the Inquisition was most concerned about, however, was the question of the validity of his inner experience. After his experiences at Manresa, Ignatius was convinced that God communicated directly with the individual person. In his *Spiritual Exercises* he would advise that 'the director of the Exercises, as a balance at equilibrium, without leaning to one side or the other, should permit the Creator to deal directly with the creature and the creature directly with the Creator'. This conviction of Ignatius was quite close to what many *alumbrados* were held to believe, but Ignatius never went so far as to claim that, because of the validity of inner experience, there was no need for the externals of Christian worship and discipline.[31] Years later (1556-1558) the Dominican theologian Melchior Cano would assert that the Society of Jesus was tainted with the heresy of *alumbradismo*. He questioned especially the fact that the same contemplative spirituality was made available to everyone in the *Spiritual Exercises*, irrespective of their vocation in life. Cano believed that it was not ultimately possible to combine active and contemplative lives. This might lead, he feared, to an abandonment of one's domestic responsibilities or, indeed, one's primary occupation, something which would eventually cause social upheaval.[32] Moreover, Cano would later rail (with the Jesuits in mind) against 'orders whose members go to and fro about the streets like other people ... an order of loungers ... given up to indolence'.[33] When Ignatius moved on to Salamanca to study later in 1527, he again came under the

---

31. O'Leary, 'The mysticism of Ignatius's, 86.

32. Ibid., p. 87.

33. Dauril Alden, *The Making of an Enterprise: the Society of Jesus in Portugal, its Empire and Beyond, 1540–1750* (Stanford: Stanford University Press, 1996), 22.

suspicion of the local Dominicans and landed back in prison for a further spell. Again he was acquitted and allowed to teach catechism but forbidden to discuss tricky matters such as the distinction between mortal and venial sins until he had completed his studies. He decided that, despite the acquittal, he had better move on once again.[34]

In 1528, Ignatius went to study at the Collège de Montaigu within the Sorbonne at Paris. The college which both Erasmus and Calvin attended had been founded by two representatives of the *Devotio Moderna* movement. Ignatius would remain in Paris for seven years and would form a circle of like-minded friends including a mystically inclined Pierre Favre (Le Fèvre) from Savoy, and a nobleman's son from Navarre called Francisco de Javier (Francis Xavier) and Spaniards such as Alfonso Salmeron and later Paschase Brouet from Picardy (incidentally, the first two Jesuits to land on Ireland's shores in 1541). Ignatius took his licentiate in 1533 and his MA in 1534.[35] Paris was to have a formative influence on Ignatius, not least in terms of his study of Thomism, the works of the early Fathers of the Church and a deep study of Scripture and particularly the letters of St Paul. Loyola by now had moved away from believing that he could gain merit through his own efforts and tended more towards an Augustinian position which stressed, rather, the all-sufficiency of divine grace. While accepting that none could be saved unless predestined to be, Ignatius was clear of the need to be cautious in how one spoke of the doctrine. In the fifteenth rule of the *Spiritual Exercises*, he notes that

---

34. O'Malley, *The First Jesuits*, 28.

35. Mullett, *The Catholic Reformation*, 85.

... if somehow the topic is brought up on occasions, it should
be treated of in such a way that the ordinary people do not
fall into an error, as sometimes happens when they say, 'It
is already determined whether I shall be saved or damned,
and this cannot now be changed by my doing good or evil.'
Through this they grow listless and neglect the works which
lead to good and to the spiritual advancement of their souls.[36]

As has frequently been observed, Ignatius's autobiographical
account of his very formative Parisian years is frustrating in
what it does not reveal. Ignatius does not mention encountering
Lutheranism in Paris nor, more surprisingly still, does he
refer to the famous Lutheranising sermon of the rector of the
university, Nicholas Cop, in 1533 (a sermon on which John
Calvin very likely collaborated). Neither does he mention 'the
affair of the placards' when, on 17 October 1534, Paris awoke to
dozens of Lutheran slogans posted across the city.

The Founding of the 'Company'

By 1534 Ignatius's group of companions decided to leave
for Jerusalem. This time they did not embark on the trip for
personal sanctification, but with a view to spending their
lives in the service of souls, of ministering to Christians living
there and converting its Muslim inhabitants.[37] They bound
themselves to this course of action by vow on 15 August 1534,
along with an additional vow to live a life of poverty. They were
to be bitterly disappointed when, eventually having met in
Venice in 1537, they found that a coalition of the Holy Roman

---

36. *Ignatius of Loyola: Spiritual Exercises and Collected Works,* ed. George
E. Ganss (Mahwah: Paulist Press, 1991), 213.

37. Mullett, *The Catholic Reformation*, 87.

Emperor Charles V, the Pope and the Venetian republic had decided to embark upon a war with the Ottoman Turks so that all commercial sailings to the Holy Land were postponed.[38] In the meantime Ignatius and five of his companions had been ordained priests. At this point, Ignatius and his group decided that they would make themselves available for whatever service the Pope required of them. By October 1537, they had decided to brand themselves the Company of Jesus (stating that they had no other superior but him). *Compagnia* meant fraternity, guild or association and was rendered in Latin as *Societas*.[39] Thus the Society of Jesus was born. Ignatius had sent nine of his company to Rome to seek papal approval for a pilgrimage to the Holy Land. Later, Pope Paul III would comment that the Jerusalem of their true vocation was, in fact, Italy.

The raison d'être of the society was not yet immediately clear. In Rome in 1538, the welcome for the Jesuits was rather mixed. The 'Company', in fact, got off to a faltering start when an initial mission to convert the city's large population of prostitutes was looked upon with some suspicion by ecclesiastical authorities.[40] Once again they were suspected of being *alumbrados* or, indeed, Lutherans in disguise, until they were declared innocent by the city governor. It is at this point that Ignatius's autobiography ends. He would spend the rest of his days in Rome. Ignatius and his company would continue to gain powerful enemies, not just in the Spanish Inquisition, which questioned his orthodoxy, but also in the person of Gian Pietro Carafa (the future Pope

---

38. MacCulloch, *Reformation*, 221.

39. Ibid., 222.

40. Ibid.

Paul IV) who, as a patriotic Neapolitan, detested Ignatius as a Spaniard under whose rule the Neapolitans lay.[41]

Carafa's hostility was ironic in ways, for the closest model for the Jesuits' developing constitution was, in fact, that of the Theatines, Carafa's non-monastic association of clerks-regular founded some years earlier. Such were the similarities that the Jesuits in the early stages were often called Theatines by outsiders (to their great annoyance, it must be added!) In fact, the Theatines approached them some years later with the offer of a merger to which the Majorcan Jesuit Jeronimo Nadal would respond: 'we are not monks – the world is our house'.[42] Matters were not helped when, in 1537, Ignatius wrote an impertinent letter of advice to Carafa on how to better organise the Theatine order. Where Ignatius did get a welcome was among a group of clergy known loosely as the *Spirituali*. Reform-minded and of a humanist bent, they appreciated the devotion of Ignatius and his companions to the interior life of the soul. One of the best known of the *Spirituali* was Cardinal Gasparo Contarini who made the *Spiritual Exercises* under Ignatius's direction in 1539. Another prominent member of the *Spirituali* was the Englishman, Reginald Pole. It was Contarini, perhaps more than any other, who was instrumental in securing Pope Paul III's approval for Ignatius's society with a bull of foundation in 1540. The Jesuits were to receive special treatment from Paul III in one important aspect: contrary to the general trend of the Council of Trent (which subjected religious orders to episcopal control), the Pope made the Jesuits exempt, allowing them free rein to administer the sacraments and to preach without the

---

41. Ibid.

42. Ibid.

permission of local bishops. The Jesuits were thus regarded as the 'Pope's men' and took a special fourth vow of obedience to him.

The Jesuits followed in the tradition of earlier orders such as the Franciscans and Dominicans to the extent that they preached and heard confessions (and later were in the vanguard of Counter-Reformation missionary ventures). They were also distinctive in significant ways. As Diarmaid MacCulloch observes, they did not adopt regular decision-making gatherings of the community in chapter; neither did they gather in daily worship 'in choir'. They refused also to develop a distinctive form of dress for their members to wear.[43] Their distinctiveness and the favour with which they were later treated often brought them into conflict with older orders such as the Franciscans. One humorous example of such antagonism can be found in the story of a heated exchange between an Irish Jesuit and an Irish Franciscan in the early seventeenth century. The Jesuit accused the Franciscan of being 'red-headed like Judas', whereupon the Franciscan retorted: 'that Judas had red hair is merely conjecture, but that he was a member of the Society of Jesus is certainly a fact!'[44]

In many respects, it might be argued that the Jesuits addressed the problem of excessive clericalism that had been exposed by the Protestant reformers. They steered clear of becoming a monastic order on the basis that Ignatius believed that it was possible to live a spiritual life within the world, and his society wanted to affirm the value of that world. This, however, was also the approach of the *Devotio Moderna* movement of the

---

43. Ibid., 224.

44. In the Middle Ages there was a traditional belief that Judas had red hair.

late fifteenth century, which had a significant effect on Ignatius. His spirituality was profoundly influenced by the classic work of the *Devotio Moderna*, *The Imitation of Christ* by Thomas à Kempis, which vigorously affirmed that the clergy had no special privileges in the eyes of God. It had become the handbook of lay dévots living in the world of work and family. Ignatius would remain, then, in MacCulloch's words, 'an extremely unclerical cleric' for his time.[45]

Some have even, perhaps a little too hastily, attributed an evangelical puritanism to Ignatius in his early years. He waged a battle to stop Jesuit churches staging elaborately sung high masses. In the original version of the Jesuit *Formula Vivendi* (their equivalent of a religious rule), following the statement that the Jesuits would not celebrate the canonical hours of prayer 'in choir', the text states that neither organs nor singing should be used at Mass for

> We have found them to be a serious impediment because, according to the design of our vocation, we must be frequently occupied during large parts of the day and sometimes even the night in consoling the sick in body and in soul, as well as in other necessary undertakings.[46]

To some members of the Roman curia, such as Cardinal Ghinucci, this risked confirming Lutherans in their criticisms of Catholic worship and so it was omitted in the official bull of approbation for the order in 1540.[47]

---

45. Ibid., 224–5.

46. O'Malley, *The First Jesuits*, 135.

47. Ibid.

Influenced by works such as Ludolf of Saxony's *Vita Jesu Christi*, the *Spiritual Exercises* of Ignatius, made with the guidance of a director, would help those meditating on biblical scenes by encouraging them to imagine the location and those present (a so-called 'application of the senses'). Ignatius was here following in the well-established late-medieval tradition of affective devotion promoted especially by the Franciscans. Loyola wished to take those doing the *Exercises* on a visual pilgrimage to the Holy Land. Although the *Spiritual Exercises* draw deeply from medieval piety, they nevertheless modified it, and in ways transcended it. It is significant that he specified that the scenes should draw their inspiration exclusively from Scripture and not from less reliable pious legends or fables, thus excising elements such as the mystical unicorn hunt, so beloved of medieval art. This was in line with what Trent would also advocate regarding the elimination of legendary elements from church sermons. Ignatius's meditations on the mysteries of the life of Christ in the *Exercises* (*los mysterios*) were, however, far more Christocentric.[48]

In addition to their support for the early Jesuits, figures from among the *Spirituali* such as Contarini and Pole also supported reform-minded theologians such as Juan de Valdes, Bernardino Ochino and Peter Martyr Vermigli and were avidly exploring what insights they might gain from northern evangelicals (Lutherans). It might be argued that, given the right conditions, this coterie might have been able to steer the Church into recognising its shortcomings and effecting a renewal of its theology as had been suggested by no less a figure than Erasmus

---

48. Mullett, *The Catholic Reformation*, 92–3.

of Rotterdam.[49] Such an irenic approach might have led not merely to a healing of the breach within Christendom, but may also have won the gratitude of Emperor Charles V who would have liked nothing better than to see peace break out in his imperial lands. What began hopefully in preparations for the Regensburg Colloquy in 1541 (which Ignatius's companion Pierre Favre attended) ended in failure and resulted in the hardening of positions. The approach of conciliation adopted by Contarini and his fellow *Spirituali* nose-dived and left the way open for hardliners such as Carafa to say 'I told you so.' As for their theologians, Valdes died in 1541 and Cardinal Contarini the following year; Bernardino Ochino, summoned to Rome, fled instead on horseback to Calvin's Geneva. He was soon followed by Peter Martyr Vermigli who ended up being welcomed to Strasbourg by the Reformer Martin Bucer. Now that Carafa's hour had come, this would not be the last flight of scholars and theologians across the Alps to the Reformed world.[50] When Carafa was elected pope as Paul IV in March 1555, Ignatius of Loyola said that his bones rattled from head to foot for fear of what might follow. He feared the worst for the Society of Jesus but his days were already numbered. By the following year he had died and Pope Paul IV used the opportunity to force the Company to surrender much of its freedom of decision making and began remodelling it along the lines of a more conventional religious order.

JUDGING IGNATIUS

So how should we regard Ignatius of Loyola? Up to some decades

---

49. MacCulloch, *Reformation*, 226.

50. Ibid., 226–31.

ago, he was regarded as a soldier saint, a militant and effective Counter-Reformation leader.[51]

Part of the reason that Ignatius continues to be regarded by many as a Counter-Reformation figure of some stature goes back to the manner in which the Society would later respond to the growing calls for a defence of Catholic doctrine and practice: Jesuits on mission would largely be seen as the Counter-Reformation's storm troopers. Another reason why Ignatius has been regarded as the *Generalissimo* of Catholic reaction is the manner in which he has been portrayed by his early biographers – figures such as Pedro de Ribadaneira towards the end of the sixteenth century, a time when the battle lines had hardened in Reformation Europe.[52] Ribadaneira's biography is marked by an aggressive stance towards Protestantism, in which Ignatius is the great soldier saint, a man of action, a John Wayne-type figure whose job is to clear the European saloon of 'heresy'. In keeping with this picture, Ribadaneira's biography played down the seriousness of the charges brought against Ignatius in Alcalá, as such details might well have sullied the reputation for orthodoxy which the Society now enjoyed. It also refrains from alluding to Ignatius's frequent difficulties with obedience.[53]

It is quite a different individual that we find in the pages of Ignatius's own autobiography which he dictated to his Jesuit friend, Luis Gonsalves da Cámara, in the 1550s. Here we find Ignatius the mystic, a man devoted to exploring the interior

---

51. See especially Ron Darwen SJ, 'Will the real Ignatius please stand up?' *Thinking Faith: the Online Journal of the British Jesuits* (30 July 2008), accessed 6 May 2011.

52. See Terence O'Reilly, 'Ignatius of Loyola and the Counter-Reformation: the hagiographic tradition', *Heythrop Journal* 31 (1990), 439–70.

53. Ibid., 453.

life and helping others to do the same, a portrait which tends to be emphasised today by members of the Society of Jesus.[54] To equate Ignatius of Loyola too closely with the Counter-Reformation cause is to misunderstand him and his founding of the Jesuits. It can be argued that without a Luther and a Calvin, there would still have been a Loyola. His motivation and that of his confrères was not principally to 'reform the church' but 'to aid souls'. Reading Ignatius's autobiography, one does not get a sense that the Reformation is raging in Europe: indeed, it is scarcely mentioned at all.[55] Ignatius and the Jesuits must be understood, then, in the much wider context of the renewal of religious life proposed by groups such as the *Devotio Moderna* of the Low Countries and the promotion of an interiorised and personal spirituality. Ignatius belongs more properly to this earlier period of reform. His formative years in Spain in the 1520s (when the works of Erasmus were becoming popular) were years in which the name of Martin Luther can have meant very little to him. Diarmaid MacCulloch in his recent survey of the history of Christianity, speaks of the founding of the Jesuits as 'a gratuitous weapon to be placed in the Pope's hand'.[56] This too is to overplay the early significance of Reformation polemic for the Society. It has sometimes been commented that in the mid to late 1530s, Ignatius and his companions wished to go to Jerusalem to 'help souls', not to Saxony to debate with them.

54. Darwen, 'Will the real Ignatius please stand up?'

55. John W. O'Malley, 'Was Ignatius Loyola a Church Reformer? How to look at early modern Catholicism', *Catholic Historical Review* 77:2 (1991), 184.

56. Diarmaid MacCulloch, *A History of Christianity: The First Three Thousand Years* (London and New York: Allen Lane, 2009), 661.

Towards the end of Ignatius's life, however, one does notice signs of a growing awareness of the necessity of defending the faith (something closer to what we have come to call the Counter-Reformation). The original wording of the bull which established the Society of Jesus stated that the community was founded 'principally for the advancement of souls in the Christian life and doctrine and for the propagation of the faith ...' Some ten years later in 1550, influenced perhaps by his correspondence with fellow Jesuits such as Peter Canisius in Germany, Ignatius revised the wording of the bull to state that the order was founded for the '*defence* and propagation of the faith'.[57] This should not wholly obscure what went before, however, nor should it dominate the principal motivations behind the founding of the Ignatius's company of Jesus. Ignatius and his followers were more properly heirs of earlier efforts to reform and renew religious life, a movement in which figures such as Desiderius Erasmus played a prominent part. Ignatius, then, is probably best regarded as saint of late-medieval mysticism and the *Devotio Moderna* rather than Counter-Reformation general.

---

57. O'Reilly, 'Ignatius of Loyola and the Counter-Reformation', 446. My emphasis.

CHAPTER 3

Jesus of Geneva: Encountering Christ with Calvin in the Gospels

Gordon Campbell

Calvin's most famous work, the *Institutes of the Christian Religion*, devotes Book 2 to Christ, dealing in sequence with the topics of the incarnation; Christ's humanity; his divine and human natures; his work as Redeemer (in the offices of prophet, priest and king); his death, resurrection and ascension; and his status as Saviour. Each of these explorations distils something of Calvin's patient and committed reading of Scripture. For the topic of this lecture, encountering Christ with Calvin in the Gospels, I propose that we turn not to the *Institutes* but to Calvin's *Commentary on the Harmony (or Concordance) of the three Synoptic Gospels*, published in 1555 in both Latin and French.[1] The *Harmony* comprises over eight hundred pages of commentary. It is not generally well-known – perhaps its length scares off potential readers! Calvin also wrote a commentary on John's Gospel, which I must leave for another time and place. I hope to walk you, as it were, through the Synoptic Gospels with

1. For this study I have used the three-volume version in English (translated from the Latin original), *A Harmony of the Gospels: Matthew, Mark and Luke*, tr. A. W. Morrison (Edinburgh: St Andrew Press, 1972) together with a nineteenth-century version of the French original by C. Meyrueis (Paris, 1854–55) available online at http://www.unige.ch/theologie/cite/calvin/CommentairesNT.html. Only references to the English edition, however, are given here.

Calvin as our guide and using his own words. Calvin's method in the *Harmony* is patterned on the efforts of his mentor, the Strasbourg Reformer Martin Bucer, which he considers to be 'beyond reproach'.[2] Calvin calls his own work 'a welcome and useful short-cut', as it spares his reader having to compare and reconcile the three Synoptic Gospels fully.[3]

In his dedicatory epistle to the burgomasters of Frankfurt and his preface to the reader, Calvin gives us a flavour of what to expect. He explains: 'I have attempted ... to magnify the progress of Christ on his four-horse chariot, like one of his attendant heralds.'[4] In speaking of the Gospels like this, Calvin acknowledges his debt to the Church Fathers he knew so well. The Four Gospels themselves are 'four narratives which describe Christ's working out of the office of Mediator'.[5] For Calvin, each Evangelist addresses the one essential point that 'Christ was that Son of God, the Redeemer promised to mankind [who] fulfilled the things that God had promised from the beginning.'[6] Here, as so often, Calvin is taking his reader to the Old Testament so that its words of promise might be kept constantly in mind and their fulfilment in Christ prove an encouragement for faith. Already in these opening quotations from the Harmony, Calvin has described Christ as the Redeemer and the Mediator. Both are characteristic terms and raise the questions, 'Who is this Mediator and Redeemer? What are his essential attributes?' My presentation of the Reformer's

---

2. *Harmony of the Gospels I*, xiv.

3. Ibid., xiii.

4. Ibid., Dedicatory Epistle, ix.

5. Ibid., xii.

6. Ibid., xii.

portrait will draw upon five major phases of the synoptic story of Jesus, up to (but not including) the events recounted by the resurrection narratives. These are:

- The infancy narratives in Matthew and Luke
- The beginning of the public ministry of Jesus
- The Sermon on the Mount (in Matthew) and on the Plain (in Luke)
- The remainder of the public ministry of Jesus, in teaching, healing and other activity
- The passion and death of Jesus.

PHASE I: THE INFANCY NARRATIVES IN MATTHEW AND LUKE

Christ is 'unique and only-begotten'.[7] In the annunciation to Mary in Luke 1, Calvin notes how the angel helps 'the holy virgin recognise that he would be the Redeemer promised of old to the fathers' (*I*, 25); his conception by the Holy Spirit attests to his divine nature and origin and therefore, his dignity and purity: he is fit to be set apart as 'the true Mediator' (*I*, 29), free of the stain of sin. In Mt 1:16's reference to 'Jesus, who is called Christ', readers glimpse 'no private individual, but one divinely anointed to fulfil the role of Redeemer' (*I*, 60). And in Mt 1:21, 'God's Son is commended to us under the name Jesus as the Author of salvation ... He is expressly called the Church's Saviour' (*I*, 65). This point is a matter of vital concern for faith:

> Christ is not recognised ... as truly our Saviour, until we learn to embrace by faith the free remission of sins and know that we are counted righteous before God, as men cleared

7. *Harmony I*, 24. For ease of reading, the following references to the *Harmony* will be inserted into the body of the text.

of our guilt. Moreover we are to seek from him the Spirit of righteousness (ibid).

In the infant Jesus, Calvin already sees the one who saves *from* sin and *for* sanctification by the Spirit; already it appears that Christ's work of redemption is not far from Calvin's mind.

Calvin explains 'Immanuel' (in Mt 1:23) as long-promised, 'personal union of God with his people' (*I*, 69). Such a relation, however, requires a mediator; symbolised in the past by the mercy seat on the ark of the covenant, now it is 'tangibly displayed to the people' in Christ, as full and final revelation contrasting what was previously partial and incomplete:

> From the beginning of the world he has performed the office of Mediator, but as all this depended on the final revelation ... he puts on the title Immanuel ... to expiate the sins of men ... [and] reconcile them to the Father, altogether to fulfil the whole calling of human salvation (ibid).

For the Reformer, Christ is only ever *Christ for us*. Thus Matthew's Magi help *us* see past a child born 'poorer and lower than any urchin of the street', while their royal gifts show *us* 'that he is the divinely ordained king' (*I*, 88) to be worshipped as our Redeemer. Although *we* may not have occasion as Simeon did to cradle Jesus in our arms, we too should see Christ 'no longer in the weakness of the flesh, but in the magnificent power of the Spirit ... absent from us in body that he may better be seen sitting at the right hand of the Father' (*I*, 92). This emphasis on a *Christ for us* exemplifies Calvin's constant concern that his reader should make a believing response to Christ – a subject to which I shall return.

PHASE 2: THE BEGINNING OF THE PUBLIC MINISTRY OF JESUS

When Jesus is baptised by John, this is the fullness of time. Christ is 'revealed to the world as Redeemer' (*I*, 112). His baptism is out of obedience to his Father – 'voluntary submission', Calvin calls it (*I*, 130) – and when the heavens open and the Spirit descends (Mt 3:16), this is 'to equip him for the fulfilment of the office of Redeemer, [endowing him] with a new power' (*I*, 131). The divine voice speaks, 'introducing our Mediator with words that praise him as the Son' and declaring himself to be a Father whose 'fatherly love must flow to us in Christ' (*I*, 132) – *Christ for us*, yet again.

Calvin's interpretation of the ensuing temptations, narrated in Matthew 4 and Luke 4, maintains the same emphasis on the career of the Redeemer. 'Christ was tempted as the Representative of all the faithful' and his use of Scripture against the tempter shows *us* how to fight and win (*I*, 137). Here, as the account of Jesus' public ministry begins, it emerges straightaway that out of *Christ for us* Calvin will also draw a Christ whom we may imitate – in this case, by our using Scripture as Jesus did to overcome temptation. Likewise when Calvin reads in Lk 6.12 that Jesus 'continued all night in prayer', he will not fail to detect another lesson for the disciple of Christ: 'If he who was full of the Holy Spirit besought the Father so warmly and urgently to be the overseer of his choice, how much greater is our need' (*I*, 165).

PHASE 3: THE SERMON ON THE MOUNT (MATTHEW) AND ON THE PLAIN (LUKE)

Confronted in Matthew 5 with the Sermon on the Mount (and in Luke 6 with Luke's Sermon on the Plain) the Reformer demonstrates an awareness of certain aims which the Evangelists had. Calvin has already highlighted what he considers to be the

Evangelists' unconcern, in Matthew 4 and Luke 4, for 'a fixed and distinct time sequence' and indeed their neglect of 'the order of days' (*I*, 155). Now he pinpoints where their real interest lies:

> Both Evangelists had the intention of gathering into one single passage the chief headings of Christ's teaching ... [in] a short summary of the teaching of Christ, gathered from many and various discourses (*I*, 168).

Calvin's exposition will continually remind his reader how the Gospel writer's compilation is 'not all to be taken as from one context' (*I*, 227) but read, instead, as 'an ordered summary of [Christ's] teaching, taken from many speeches' (*I*, 232). Calvin finds the objective of both Evangelists, in assembling doctrine thematically in these artificial sermons, to be thoroughly congenial and suited to his own purposes: 'I prefer,' he says, 'to take account of teaching rather than occasion, for it is a great help to our understanding to gather into one context matters which have a like significance' (*I*, 234).

This revealing remark helps explain why, in Calvin's exposition of the Synoptic Gospels, Christ's *person* is largely secondary to his *teaching*, as the following example shows. The Christ of the Sermon on the Mount or the Plain revives the Law by the Spirit, restoring God's Old Covenant word to its purity:

> Christ is not to be made into a new Law-giver, adding anything to the everlasting righteousness of his Father, but is ... a faithful Interpreter, teaching us the nature of the Law, its object and its scope.[8]

---

8. *Harmony I*, 83–4; the comment relates to Mt 5:21ff.

For Calvin, we may say, the Christ of the Sermon essentially stands guarantor for the ethical use to which the Law is to be put in structuring the life of the fledgling Reformed Church and that of its members.

Of course, such a compendium of Jesus' teaching as the Sermon on the Mount cannot fail to offer the disciple an example to follow. Again prayer emerges as an aspect of spiritual life for which, Calvin observes, Jesus is the model. The Lord's Prayer, found in both Sermons (Mt 6:9-13 and Lk 11:1-4), is, for Calvin, not so much a formula to be repeated verbatim, although in his liturgy he was quite happy to use it in this way. Rather, this prayer is a means 'to direct and control our vows, that they should not wander beyond these limits'. In prayer it is not the actual words that matter, but the matters put into word (*I*, 205).

PHASE 4: THE REMAINDER OF THE PUBLIC MINISTRY OF JESUS (TEACHING, HEALING, OTHER ACTIVITY)

In this phase Jesus the teacher remains in focus. In Mt 13 Jesus explains to his Apostles the enigmatic parable of the sower (Mt 13:16): Their enlightened eyes

> ... perceive the glory worthy of the only begotten Son of God and acknowledge that he is their Redeemer, because the lively image of God shines upon them and in it they perceive their salvation and full blessedness (*I*, 68).

Both Jesus' teaching *and* his miracles, however, constitute mighty works: 'Christ was not dumb while he was showing ... the power of the Father. In fact the miracles were joined to the Gospel so as to draw attention to the voice of Christ' (*I*, 16); thus 'the power of the Holy Spirit shines splendidly in all Christ's words and deeds' (*II*, 39). Furthermore, the miracles have 'the deliberate purpose of proving him to be the Son of God and the Redeemer given to the world' (*II*, 35).

We might wonder how Calvin balances the humanity and the divinity of Jesus. Sometimes, the *human* side of Calvin's Jesus is prominent. In Luke's infancy narrative we read that 'the child [Jesus] grew' (Lk 2:40); says Calvin, 'Christ according to his human nature increased in the free gifts of the Holy Spirit, that from his fullness he might shower them upon us, for we draw grace from his grace' (*II*, 106). In Mt 8:1-4, the man Jesus touches a leper and for the Reformer this is no wonder, since 'he willed to put on our flesh in order that he might cleanse us from all our sins' (*I*, 244). When, in the next episode, Jesus marvels at the faith of the centurion (Mt 8:10), this also makes sense 'inasmuch as he had taken on our human emotions, along with our flesh' (*I*, 249-50). A similar point is made at the feeding of the five thousand (Mt 14). Like his disciples, Jesus is exhausted by the crowd; nevertheless, whenever 'the demands of his office called him to a new task, he willingly put aside his own needs and set himself to teach the crowds' (*II*, 147).

At other times, Calvin sees the *divine* nature of Jesus to the fore. In all three Gospels, the healing of the paralysed man (Mt 9:1-8/Mk 2:1-12/Lk 5:17-26) has 'exceptional glory' within it (*I*, 257), since 'all [are] struck with wonder, so as to be made to give glory to God' (*I*, 260) – all, that is, but the scribes who are thinking that only God can remit sins. Jesus knows their thoughts (e.g. Mt 9:4; Mt 12:25/Lk 11:16), which for Calvin is 'an instance of his Godhead' (ibid). Calvin's exegesis of Jesus' encounter with the Canaanite/Syrophoenician woman (Mt 15:21-28/Mk 7:24-30) is especially interesting. Mark recounts how Jesus came to Tyre/Sidon secretly but, says Calvin, 'by his divine Spirit Christ foresaw what would happen'; and when Christ responds to the woman's request with silence (Mt 15:23), this is because 'there are two ways in which Christ speaks and is silent ... [for] he spoke inwardly to the woman's mind and so this secret instinct stood in place of the external preaching' (*II*, 167).

At still other times, Calvin sees *both* of Christ's natures or 'both sides of his mediatorial office' (*II*, 151) in play, as in the case of the calming of the storm (Mt 14:22-33/Mk 6:45-52). As Son of God he knew a storm was coming but did not prevent it, thus preparing for the miracle to follow. Yet at the same time he also 'showed himself man by praying' (ibid). In the healing of the deaf and dumb man, too (Mt 15:29-39/Mk 7:31-8:10), there is the *divine*, in that 'the faculty of speech [restored to the man] flows from himself alone', and he can open deaf ears; but equally there is the *human*, as reflected in '[Christ's] singular love towards men when he so much sympathised with their miseries' (*II*, 173). Calvin is always careful to defend both Christ's humanity and his deity: tamper with the latter and you reduce 'his power to save us'; touch his humanity, and you close 'our familiar way of approach to him' (*III*, 42).

Christ for us is never far from the Reformer's thoughts, as for example when he handles the call of Levi/Matthew: 'Why was Christ himself made a propitiation, and a curse, unless it was to stretch out a hand to accursed sinners?' (*I*, 264).

Christ came precisely to call sinners – *sinners like us* – to repentance (e.g. Mt 9:13). Similarly, when Jesus dines at Simon the Pharisee's house (Lk 7:36-50), Simon himself may 'not know that [Christ] is the Mediator whose proper office is to bring back unhappy sinners to favour with God' – but Calvin knows, and so do *we* his readers: 'Christ was given as the Liberator of wretched and lost men, to restore them from death to life' (*II*, 85).

A constant goal of Calvin's exposition is that 'we should learn to look at Christ with the eyes of faith' (*II*, 56). In Mt 11:27-30, declaring that all things have been delivered to him, Christ calls the weary to come to him for rest. Says Calvin, Christ is here inviting people

> ... to come straight to him and seek assurance of salvation in him ... life is opened up to us in Christ himself ... although our salvation is always hidden in God, yet Christ is the conduit through whom it flows to us and is received by our faith, so that it is firm and certain in our hearts.

Therefore, Calvin concludes, we must not swerve from Christ (*II*, 85). This emphasis on putting our trust in the Saviour for our salvation is nowhere clearer, it seems to me, than at Caesarea Philippi (Mt 16:13-19/Mk 8:27-29/Lk 9:18-20). There Peter answers Jesus' question 'Who do you say I am?' (Mt 16:15), identifying Christ as 'the Redeemer ... come forth from heaven marked with the anointing of God'. For Calvin this answer 'contains the whole sum of our salvation' (*II*, 185) and he does not fail to instruct his reader fully in all that Peter must mean!

> In the praise of Christ is comprehended his eternal kingdom and priesthood, that he reconciles God to us and wins perfect righteousness, expiating our sins by his sacrifice, that he keeps his own, whom he has received into his trust and care, and adorns and enriches us with every kind of blessing (ibid).

We may profitably feature one last episode from the public ministry of Jesus – the transfiguration (Mt 17:1-8/Mk 9:2-8/Lk 9:28-36). Here the Reformer detects Christ's majesty hidden under the weakness of the flesh; his glory would not manifest itself till his resurrection, but meantime '[Christ] kept entire his deity, even if it was hidden under the veil of his flesh' (*II*, 202). Therefore, on the mountain the three disciples got a 'partial taste' of his infinite glory, seeing his face shine like the sun; however 'now [since his ascension] it far transcends the sun's glory' (*II*, 198).

PHASE 5: THE PASSION AND DEATH OF JESUS

Jesus' final days at Jerusalem begin with the triumphal entry, and what Calvin sees as 'a rabble tearing down branches, strewing their clothes on the road, giving the empty name of King to Christ' (*II*, 293). But even this is *for us*: Christ who *now* sits as universal king at God's right hand *still* 'appoints from his heavenly throne obscure men to celebrate his majesty in their lowly manner!' *(II*, 294). Like the people's joy that day, *our joy* is in 'the intervention of the Mediator ... the one who frees his people from all evils' (*II*, 292). Their acclamation 'blessed is the kingdom of our father David' prefigures *our* own prayer 'thy kingdom come', in which we ask God 'to keep his Son as our king' (*II*, 294).

As the passion narrative unfolds, Calvin's commentary becomes dominated by a sense of the approaching fulfilment of Christ's mission and office. When he cleanses the Temple, Jesus is 'testifying to himself as King and High Priest, who presides over the temple and worship of God' (*III*, 3–4). Healing in the Temple courts, Jesus proves that he owns the rights and privileges of Messiah (*III*, 6). In the parable of the wicked tenants (Mt 21:33–46/ Mk 12:1-12/Lk 20:9-19), Christ speaks like the prophets before him and foreshadows his imminent death, while his perception of his opponents' evil intent (Mt 22:18) discloses his divinity.

The last of Christ's predictions of his death (Mt 26:1/Mk 14:1) shows *both* 'that the Son of God went to face death of his own will, to reconcile the world to the Father' and also 'that he purposely came to Jerusalem to seek to meet death there' (*III*, 119-20). As death approaches (Mt 26:18) Christ is presented, by Calvin, as being eager to accomplish his Father's will. In spite of this there is also Gethsemane (Mt 26:36-44/Mk 14:32-40/Lk 22:39-46), with all its panic and anguish. Ambrose of Milan had said, 'I boldly speak of this sorrow, because I preach his cross.' Calvin approves, adding with Cyril of Alexandria, that Christ's fear in the very presence of death fulfils 'the Redeemer's role of suffering ... as truly man' – though, Calvin goes on, 'pure and unsullied ... without any spot of sin (*III*, 148). So, as Jesus prays for the cup if possible to pass from him, we witness his human struggle to bow to the Father's will, when 'the terror of death fell on him and darkness covered him ... [and] for a moment he did not think how he was sent to be the Redeemer of the human race' (*III*, 150-1).

A terror greater than death here terrifies Christ in his human nature, namely, a 'sight of the dread tribunal of God' and the weight of 'our sins, whose burden was laid on him' (*III*, 148). But he fights and overcomes, and this too was *for us*: 'He wished to wrestle in anguish, in painful and hard combat, that in his own person he might win the victory for us' (*III*, 156). Calvin persists in asking his reader to apply the hermeneutic *Christ for us*. Seeing him spat upon and abused, following the hearing before Caiaphas (Mt 26:62-68/Mk 14:60-65/Lk 22:63-71) *we* should reflect on how, in God's providence, 'the face of Christ marred with spittle and blows has restored to *us* [italics mine] that image which sin corrupted, indeed destroyed' (*III*, 168). Through the Jewish verdict reached (Mt 27:1), 'the Son of God had to be condemned ... by an earthly judge, so that *we* [italics mine] might clear our guilt in heaven' (*III*, 174). Considering Jesus as he stands before Pilate 'in sad and cheap array ... *we* shall take grounds for confidence from it, that relying on his intercessions *we* [italics mine] may come before [God] happy and eager' (III, 179, cf. Mt 27:11-14 / Mk 15:2-5 / Lk 23:2-12)

Christ's sufferings (Mt 27:24-32/Mk 15:15-22/Lk 23:24-32) ought to make us reflect on what he endured on our behalf and what he obtained for us. Thus as we see Pilate condemn Jesus (innocent though he is) and wash his hands of the matter, Calvin deduces that

> God wished his Son's innocence attested in this way, that it might be more clear that our sins were condemned in him ... the penalty that was due to us was laid on Christ; now with the guilt removed, let us not hesitate to advance into the sight of the heavenly Judge (*III*, 187-8).

Indeed, as we watch an innocent man being handed over for crucifixion we should reflect that 'unless [Christ] had gone bail for us and undergone the penalty we deserved, we should still be involved in the guilt of our crimes' (*III*, 188-9). As for the soldiers' mistreatment of Jesus, Calvin sees beyond its foul ugliness to 'God's inestimable mercy ... in lowering his only-begotten Son to these depths, for our sake' (*III*, 189), because, in that very abasement, where he is 'placed lower than a robber and a murderer', Christ wins 'an ascent for us into the heavenly glory. Thus he was reckoned worse than a thief to bring us into the company of angels' (*III*, 183-4).

Finally, we may sample a few of Calvin's comments on what the cross means for us (Mt 27:33-38/Mk 15:21-28/Lk 23:33-

34, 38). 'The Evangelists,' he says, 'portray the Son of God as stripped of his clothes that we may know the wealth gained for us by this nakedness, for it shall dress us in God's sight ... his raiment ... torn apart like booty [makes] us rich with the riches of his victory' (*III*, 194). Faced with Christ's incomparable love for us, should not we (Calvin reasons) emulate the penitent thief who, as death closes in (Lk 23:35-37, 39-43), 'adores Christ as King ... celebrates his reign in the fearful and unspeakable loss, and proclaims him Author of life in the hour of dying'? (*III*, 198-9).

Such is the Christ we meet in Calvin's commentary on the Synoptic Gospels. What, then, are we to make of Calvin's Redeemer? Five issues, it seems to me, are worthy of our consideration, whether or not we are disciples of Calvin. Like 'Calvin', all five points begin with 'C'.

COMMITMENT

It is my joy and privilege to be *both* a Christian minister and our denomination's professor of New Testament studies. In the Academy, as distinct from the Church, Biblical Studies in the twentieth century could often be rather dry, detached and horizontal (devoid of a transcendent dimension), instead of committed, impassioned and vertical. However, today input from self-consciously Christian scholars is once more welcome. In this regard I must say that I find Calvin's exegetical work refreshingly current. Energetic exegesis matters, for out of the interpretation of God's self-revelation all theology springs. I confess that Calvin's *engagement*[9] has inspired me. This remains the case even when I think he may have missed the point of a

---

9. In its French sense of 'coming to grips with'.

given text - for example, when he is oblivious to the unique contribution of the inspired Evangelist - or whenever his prose brims with the drama or venom of controversies which, like sleeping dogs, we should probably let lie.

For my second 'C' I shall express a certain dissatisfaction, not just with Calvin, but with ourselves and our situation.

CONGLOMERATION

Whilst we should not penalise Calvin for lacking the insights or falling short of the standards of contemporary Gospel scholarship, we ought nonetheless to see Calvin's limitations and to learn any lessons arising. One such lesson is the lack of interest on Calvin's part, in the *Commentary on the Harmony*, in Matthew's Jesus, or Mark's, or Luke's (or for that matter, John's). I am exercised by the fact that four distinct Jesus portraits, all of them inspired, are bequeathed to us by the Gospel canon. By implication, these four ought to be as irreducible for us as they are inseparable. I reckon that we all, like Calvin, reduce four down to one but that we may not be nearly as careful as Calvin was, in arriving at our synthesis. Is not the Jesus of many Christians and their leaders, today, more of an unholy conglomeration drawn haphazardly from the Gospel according to saint Amalgam, a kind of hotchpotch or 'DIY Jesus'? To my mind, the Church - for her worship and preaching, her teaching and outreach - needs more than ever to gaze long and hard at each Gospel portrait of Jesus and at all four. While Calvin may not help us to do so directly, indirectly his sustained and careful dialogue with the Gospel text should be our inspiration.

My third and fourth 'C's, indissoluble from one another, are taken together.

CHRIST FOR US AND IN US AND CONFIDENCE IN CHRIST

I have tried to suggest that *Christ for us* is perhaps the chief characteristic of the portrait Calvin paints. But for Calvin, whatever may be said objectively about the Jesus of Gospel testimony is meaningless unless and until it is appropriated by his reader as subjective truth. Constantly taken up though Calvin is with how Christ achieved salvation *for us*, he remains no less concerned with how that salvation becomes effective *in us*. Indeed, it is out of the *for us* that the *in us* inevitably springs. Accordingly, Calvin's mediator, who reconciles man to God, is not merely to be known in some detached fashion but may be entrusted with your life. Calvin's redeemer is no hero to be admired from afar, but a welcoming, personal Saviour. Reformed theology has therefore spoken of a salvation *accomplished,* necessarily implying a salvation *applied* or *appropriated*.

In short, for Calvin the Gospels must also become Gospel, through the enlivening work of the Holy Spirit. Calvin's Christ, now ascended to glory, has achieved *for* the believer all that is necessary for salvation, and therefore *in* the believer there is manifested a consequent assurance and confidence for living a life of faith, from day to day, under the lordship of the glorified Christ. Such confidence or faith is no state of certainty, free of all doubt, amounting to presumption (for Calvin, at least). Instead, it is a quiet and intimate knowing Christ and being known by him, in the power of the Spirit. In Ireland today, where the Gospel risks being deemed every bit as flawed as the Church, is this not precisely a Christ for our times, a Christ whose relevance *for* people may and must be measured by the change that knowing him by faith actually produces *in* people?

This brings me quite naturally to my fifth and final 'C'.

CHRISTLIKENESS

Whenever there is a lesson of Christian discipleship to be drawn from Christ's words or actions, Calvin will do so all the way to the cross, as I have tried to show. For all that Christ is our unique redeemer and mediator, who in every particular has won our salvation for us alone and unaided, in Calvin's eyes the Jesus of the Gospel testimony remains an example for the Christian disciple to follow. This is a constantly recurring emphasis in the *Harmony* which locates Calvin, fair and square, within the tradition of the imitation of Christ. A largely overlooked aspect of Calvin's Jesus, it is also a part of the Reformer's exegetical theology. In my Presbyterian tradition, and especially in Reformed ethics, this emphasis has considerable potential for re-energising a truly Christ-imitating lifestyle among Reformed Christians in our day. What benefit there may be for non Presbyterians is not for me to say, but in thinking of you, I do wonder if this re-discovery alone might be sufficient to free Calvin to speak to you in your own tradition with new relevance, perhaps drawing Catholic and Reformed into a fruitful dialogue on this and other aspects of Calvin's Christ.

CHAPTER 4

A Roman Catholic Reads Calvin on John's Gospel

Brendan McConvery

'May the Lord grant that we study the heavenly mysteries of his wisdom, making true progress in religion to his glory and our up-building.' That prayer was, I believe, often recited by John Calvin at the beginning of his lectures on the Scriptures, so it might be a place from which we can begin our work today. Let me make it clear at the outset that I make no claims for any expertise in the complex field of the study of the commentaries of Calvin. What I am attempting to do here is to describe my response as a Catholic reader of one particular commentary of John Calvin, and one perhaps not always read with the same depth of concentration.

WHY SHOULD A CATHOLIC READ CALVIN'S COMMENTARY?
Why should I read Calvin's commentary anyway? When I suggested at one of our planning meetings that I might take this as the subject for a presentation at the conference, I think I saw Ken Newell register (just for a moment) a slight hesitation as if to say, 'I wonder has he any idea of what lies in store for him when he starts reading?' To be honest, my previous familiarity with *Calvin's Commentaries* was relatively brief. I occasionally consulted them when I wanted examples of historical exegesis on certain topics, but I cannot say that I read them with a

great degree of concentration. Reckoning with Calvin over a somewhat longer period of time in preparation of this paper has been an instructive experience.

One of the challenges that faces us as we begin to speak seriously in inter-church dialogue is how do we read one another's classics? The American Roman Catholic theologian David Tracy has made the idea of a theological 'classic' central to his work. For Tracy, a classic is a person, text, event, even a melody or a symbol, encountered in some cultural experience that bears a certain excess of meaning, as well as certain timelessness. A classic confronts and provokes us in our present horizon with the feeling that something other might be the case. The encounter with a classic is an invitation to join a conversation, but the text will become a classic for the reader

> only if the reader is willing to allow that present horizon to be vexed, provoked, challenged by the claim to attention of the text itself. The provocation to present complacency often comes through the form itself (e.g. a genre) for only through a specific form is the subject matter produced *as* a provocation [italics in original], to think these questions anew.[1]

That is a rather dense statement, so let me try to unpack three aspects of it.

1. The first aspect is that we continue to read the classics because a single reading does not drain them of meaning. There is always something more to be discovered in another reading. Have you noticed, for example, how often the great classics of English literature continue to provide the

---

1. David Tracy, *The Analogical Imagination: Christian Theology and the Culture of Pluralism* (London: SCM, 1981), 105.

television stations with yet another blockbuster for a Sunday evening?

2. The second aspect is that classics provoke in us the feeling that something other might be the case. In other words, they challenge us to look beyond our present horizons, they threaten to expand them, if not even tear them apart! Classics are dangerous pieces of literature. That might be even truer of theological classics than we think. They invite us to look beyond the horizons we set to our organised and tidy world.

3. The third aspect of classics is how deeply and permanently they form the perceptions and worldview of their readers and that is precisely one of the reasons why, in dialoguing with our brothers and sisters from other faith traditions, we need to read their classics and to be prepared to enter with their creators into their worldview, laying aside any tendency to judge or find them inadequate.

It is not always easy to enter into each other's classics. If we want to do so, we may well need to learn a certain discipline. In the dedicatory letter addressed to the Senate of Geneva at the beginning of his John commentary, Calvin states that one of the purposes of his commentary is to be a 'clear witness that the Papacy is nothing but a monstrosity produced from the innumerable deceptions of Satan and that what they call the Church is more confused than Babylon'.[2] That may be one

---

2. 'The Dedicatory Epistle' in *The Gospel According to John 1-10 in John Calvin's Commentaries*, tr. T.H.L. Parker, ed. by David W. Torrance and Thomas F. Torrance (Edinburgh: St Andrew Press, 1959), 3. This, and the second volume, *The Gospel According to John (11-21) and the First Epistle of John*, same series (1961) are the sources for the quotations from Calvin cited in this article.

of the sentences Ken Newell suspected I might encounter in the commentary and which might prove an obstacle to my continuing, so let me just add it would not be the last! It does however alert us to one of the first challenges of reading classics: how can we fold back time and put ourselves with some measure of sympathy in the shoes of the writer and his intended audience? Reading through Calvin on John, I had to remind myself that I am not re-fighting the battles of the first and most bitter period of the Reformation. Those battles are over and done with. They were tragic, angry battles that left a heritage of pain that lasted for centuries. Calvin, as a man with a distinguished classical education behind him, has a fine line in invective or vituperatio. Vituperatio has, of course, a long and respectable parentage in the rhetorical handbooks of antiquity.[3] As a form of rhetorical disputation, it was not concerned with dispassionately setting out of points of disagreement for an irenic conversation, but a carefully orchestrated use of language for the purpose of winning an argument, and this was an argument Calvin was determined to win at all costs. Neither was the vituperation all on one side and Catholic polemicists gave every bit as much as they took![4]

Calvin and the other Reformers shared, along with their Catholic opponents, a profound sense of the tragic divisions

---

3. According to the *Rhetoric of Alexander* of Anaximes of Lampsacus (c. 380–320 bc), there were seven species of oratory – exhortation and dissuasion, encomium and vituperation, prosecution and defence and examination. Cf. George A. Kennedy, *Classical Rhetoric in its Christian and Secular Traditions from Ancient Times to the Modern Era* (Chapel Hill: University of Carolina Press, 1999), 24.

4. In his *Dialogue on Heresy*, for example, Thomas More berated Martin Luther as a 'pimp, an apostate, a rustic, and a friar' and William Tyndale as 'a babbler, and a devil's ape'.

of the Body of Christ but they felt they had no alternative but to adopt the course of action they took. In some sense, Irish Catholics today might be in a better position to share something of the sense of frustration they experienced of a Church in need of reform and new life, as well as the frustrating sense that the battle to reform the Church was a bitter and a costly one.

CALVIN AS A COMMENTATOR ON THE SCRIPTURES

Our first step is to try to grasp something of the extraordinary sweep of John Calvin's output as a Bible commentator and its originality. Gordon Cambell has done that splendidly in his contribution to this conference.[5] Calvin was a product of the Renaissance. His first foray into commenting on an ancient text was not on a biblical book but it was rather a commentary on a Latin classical text, the *De Clementia* of the Roman writer Seneca (4 BCE-65 CE). It was completed in 1533 when Calvin was still only in his early twenties. Twenty years later (1553) his commentary on John appeared.[6] He was now at the height of his career, with a series of commentaries on the Letters of Paul behind him. As one reads through his commentaries, what shines through most strikingly is the degree to which John Calvin appears in its pages a teacher of a community that he leads to encounter the Word of God in Scripture.

---

5. Gordon Campbell, 'Jesus of Geneva: Encountering Christ with Calvin in the Gospels', chapter 3 of the present work.

6. Quotations here are taken from *The Gospel According to John 1-10 in John Calvin's Commentaries*, tr. T. H. L. Parker, ed. by David W. Torrance and Thomas F. Torrance (Edinburgh: St Andrew Press, 1959) and *The Gospel According to John (11-21) and the First Epistle of John* in the same series (1961).

Calvin is not starting from scratch of course. He draws on the great tradition of the Fathers that has gone before him.[7] Reading through the commentary on John, it is evident that Augustine, of all the Fathers, is his greatest teacher. Yet he is not always cowed by Augustine. In his commentary on the piercing of the side of the crucified Jesus (John 19:34), for example, he has a little swipe at 'the childish invention of the Papists' who manufacture the name 'Longinus' for the soldier from the late Latin word *longē* (lance).[8] He turns then to what he considers the sense of the text with its references to water and blood. It is a sign that 'Christ brought with him the true atonement and the true washing.' Calvin continues that the sacraments which Christ left his Church have the same end: 'in baptism is shown us the purgation and purity of the soul, consisting in newness of life' and that the Supper, 'is the pledge of a perfect atonement'. He then adds:

> for this reason, I do not object to Augustine writing that our sacraments have flowed from Christ's side. For when baptism and the Holy Supper lead us to Christ's side, that by faith we may draw from him as a well what they figure, we are truly washed of our pollutions and renewed to a holy life and live before God, redeemed from death and delivered from condemnation.[9]

---

7. For Calvin's use of the Fathers, see Anthony N. S. Lane, *John Calvin: Student of the Fathers of the Church* (Edinburgh: T & T Clark, 1999). Lane suggests that 'Calvin's use of the fathers is primarily, but not exclusively, polemical' (28) and that he cites them, not as a detached modern scholar might, 'but as a polemicist, in the heat of battle' (52–3).

8. Calvin, *Gospel According to John* (11-21), 185.

9. Ibid., 186.

It may appear surprising to the modern student that Calvin began his series of commentaries on the Gospels with John, rather than with the synoptic tradition. In the preface to that commentary, he notes that, while all the Gospel writers had the same object in view, namely to show forth Christ,

> the first three exhibit his body, if I may be permitted to put it like that, but John shows forth his soul. For this reason, I am accustomed to say that this Gospel is the key to open the door of understanding to the others. For whoever grasps the power of Christ as is here graphically portrayed, will afterwards read with advantage what the others relate about the manifested Redeemer.[10]

SIGNS OF CONVERGENCE: CALVIN AND RECENT CATHOLIC EXEGESIS IN DIALOGUE

One will scarcely expect to find in a classical commentary solutions to questions that are the substance of the modern historical critical method and which have made their particular contribution to the theology and life of Christian Churches today. I suspect that when the history of ecumenical relations in the twentieth century comes to be full written, it will highlight that one of the most important areas in which the Churches have come together over the past half-century or so has been in their common concern for the Bible. Biblical study, whether done in the scholarly academy or the more immediately pastoral setting, does not recognise denominational boundaries as being impermeable, and let me pay tribute here to the enormous enrichment that Catholic scholars, who were comparatively

---

10. 'The Theme of the Gospel of John' in *Gospel According to John (1-10)*, 6.

late starters in modern academic biblical study, received from their Protestant brethren as they struggled to catch up with the explosion of biblical scholarship in the twentieth century.[11] As Roman Catholic scholarship became more assured of its voice in the modern academy, it began to repay the debt. Raymond Brown, who probably ranks as the most prolific and creative Catholic scholar writing in English of his generation, was for almost thirty years a professor at the Presbyterian Union College in New York. Let me illustrate the fruitfulness of this exchange by attempting to bring Calvin the commentator on John into dialogue with contemporary Catholic scholarship on the interpretation of two particular sections of the Fourth Gospel where lines of denominational interpretation seem to be very firmly drawn.

i. The Marriage Feast at Cana, the first of the signs of Jesus (John 2:1-11)

Traditional Catholic devotional and homiletic readings of this text have tended to place the emphasis on the role played in the narrative by the Mother of Jesus (note that John never uses her name, Mary). Particularly as preached in liturgy and meditated upon in popular devotion, it became a primary text for the theology of her place in the story of salvation and especially the theological justification of prayer through Mary's intercession. Such a limited reading however was defective. It lost sight of this little pericope's place within the overall structure of the Gospel

---

11. For a brief but accurate outline history of the emergence of Roman Catholic critical scholarship in the twentieth century, see John S. Kselman and Ronald D. Witherup, 'Modern New Testament Criticism' in *The New Jerome Biblical Commentary*, eds. R.E. Brown, Joseph A. Fitzmeyer and Roland Murphy (London: Geoffrey Chapman, 1990), 1131-45, sections 71-6 are particularly relevant.

of John. The function of Cana at the beginning of the Gospel, it
has been suggested, is a key to how we might read the signs in the
rest of the Gospel.[12] Its significance is primarily soteriological
(that is, it tells us in the abundant gift of wine, something about
the abundance of God's salvation), Christological and revelatory
('he revealed his glory and his disciples believed in him', 2:11).
The role of the Mother of Jesus must then be seen within the
larger context of the Fourth Gospel. The Mother of Jesus
appears in only two scenes in this Gospel, at Cana and Calvary,
the anticipation of 'the hour' ('my hour is not yet come', 2:4)
and the fullness of the hour of his glorification on the cross.
She is associated in both with the community of Jesus in the
process of formation – with the disciples who accompany him to
Cana, and with the group at the foot of the cross. The German
exegete Rudolph Schnackenburg, who has produced a massive
three-volume commentary on John, is probably representative
of contemporary Roman Catholic scholarship when he sums
up how Fourth Evangelist 'clearly intended to portray her as
a believing tranquil servant of her son'.[13] A Roman Catholic
reader will want to know how Calvin handles the Cana pericope.
Let me quote part of his commentary on 2:5:

> Here the Holy Virgin shows an example of the true obedience
> she owed to her Son in matters, not of human duties but of his
> divine power. Therefore she modestly acquiesces in Christ's
> reply, and exhorts others to obey his will ... But if you look

12. Raymond F. Collins: 'Cana (John 2:1-11): The first of his signs or the
key to his signs?' *Irish Theological Quarterly*, 1980, Vol. 47, No. 2 (June
1980), 79-95.

13. Rudolph Schnackenburg, *The Gospel According to St John*, Vol. 1
(London: Burns and Oates, 1980), 327.

into her intention, her statement has a wider application. For she first disclaims and lays aside the power she seems to have usurped and then she ascribes all power to Christ alone when she tells them to follow his command. Hence we are taught here in general that if we desire anything from Christ, we shall not obtain our prayers unless we depend entirely on him, look on him and in short, do whatever he commands. But he does not send us away to his mother, he invites us to himself.[14]

While Calvin's final sentence appears to reject very firmly the Catholic tradition of prayer through Mary's intercession, there is nonetheless a striking convergence between how a modern Catholic exegete like Schnackenburg can describe the Mother of Jesus in this scene as 'a believing tranquil servant of her Son' and Calvin's description of her as 'the holy virgin who shows an example of true obedience'.

ii. John Chapter 6

Roman Catholic readers of the Fourth Gospel often use the term 'eucharistic chapter' in speaking about John 6. It is a complex chapter and, from the perspective of source and compositional study of the Fourth Gospel, it is one that raises many interesting and probably insoluble questions. I do not intend to address them at length here, interesting as they might be. The contents of the chapter are well known: the Johannine form of the feeding of the multitude with loaves and fishes, the incident in which Jesus walks on the water and the lengthy sermon or teaching in the synagogue at Capernaum leading to what might be called a crisis of discipleship when Jesus asks his disciples if they also mean to

---

14. Calvin, *John 1-10*, 48.

go away. The walking on the water incident is sometimes seen as something of a foreign body in the composition of John 6, or as an incident that can only be related in a very general way to the surrounding material.

The American scholar, John P. Meier, in the second volume of his study of Jesus and the Gospel tradition, *A Marginal Jew*, reflects a common tendency among Catholic interpreters of John 6 to see the Eucharist as the unifying centre of this chapter. Summarising the results of his form and redactional study of the walking on the water incident (Jn 6:16-21), he writes:

> To a small Church struggling in the night of a hostile world and feeling bereft of Christ's presence, the walking of Christ on the water likewise symbolised the experience of Christ's presence in the Eucharist. Once again, with all the power of Yahweh bestriding the chaos of a rebellious creation, Jesus reveals himself in a secret epiphany to his frightened beleaguered disciples telling them 'It is I, fear not.' The story of the walking on the water reflects the fact that for the early church, the Eucharist was the ritualised experience of an epiphany of the risen Jesus, coming to a small group of believers labouring in the night of this present age: once again, he gave courage and calmed fears simply by announcing his presence.[15]

As a Catholic reader, I am struck by the way in which Calvin seems to avoid giving much prominence to the Eucharist in his reading of this chapter. Most modern commentators, for example, notice the echo of what was probably an early

---

15. John P. Meier, *A Marginal Jew: Rethinking the Historical Jesus*, Vol. 2, 'Mentor, Message, and Miracle' (New York: Doubleday, 1984), 923.

eucharistic liturgy in description of Jesus' action of feeding the crowd: 'he took the loaves, gave thanks, and distributed them to those who were reclining, and also as much of the fish as they wanted' (Jn 6:11) and the careful gathering of the broken pieces at the end of the meal. For Calvin, the multiplication scene provides a moral instruction that Christ has once more taught us by his example that we should begin our meals with prayer, for all those things that God has appointed for our use summon us to praise him as symbols of his infinite goodness and fatherly love towards us and that the gathering of the fragments is an exhortation to frugality.

Reading more deeply into the commentary, especially on the discourse in the synagogue at Capernaum, it is possible to see a larger view come into perspective. I suspect he may have feared that Catholic practice of the Eucharist had in some respects undermined the deeper feeding of Christ, the bread of life. 'When we hear that Christ is the bread by which our souls must be fed, it sinks deeper into our minds than if Christ had simply said that he is our life' or again that 'Christ is our bread when we come hungry to him that he may fill us.'

Moreover those who infer from this passage that the eating of Christ is nothing but faith do not reason carefully enough. I certainly acknowledge that we eat Christ in no other way than by believing. But the effect of the eating is the effect and fruit of faith itself. For faith does not look at Christ merely from afar, but embraces him, that he may become ours and dwell in us. It causes us to be united to his body, to have life in common with him and in short, to be one with him. It is therefore true that we eat Christ by faith alone, as long as we grasp how faith unites us to him.[16]

---

16. Calvin, *John 1-10*, 166.

At one point in the commentary (on verse 54), Calvin says that it is wrong to expound this whole passage as applying to the Lord's Supper. The Lord is treating the perpetual eating of his flesh through faith, but he adds:

> I confess that there is nothing said here that is not figured and actually presented to believers in the Lord's Supper. Indeed, we might say that Christ intended the Holy Supper to be the seal of this discourse. This is also the reason why John makes no mention of the Lord's Supper.[17]

Let us resume briefly the dialogue between Calvin and recent Catholic exegesis. Raymond Brown in his commentary on John, stresses the complexity of Capernaum discourse.[18] The Johannine symbol of the 'bread of life' as John understands it, is a more multi-faceted symbol than the eucharistic bread alone. It draws richly on the language of the Old Testament Wisdom literature. Like Wisdom, Jesus offers to satisfy the deepest hungers and thirsts of the human beings when he invites them to come to him. The first part of the discourse (26-50) is dominated by the idea that Jesus is the bread which has come down from heaven. In the second part (51-58), the eucharistic theme, with its echoes of the Synoptic and Pauline Last Supper accounts becomes more dominant. Since John's Gospel includes no account of an institution of the Eucharist, it is possible that this section contains his community's form of the eucharistic words (in 51b and 55). Once again, it is interesting to note the convergence between recent Catholic Johannine study and the insights of Calvin.

---

17. Ibid., 170.

18. Raymond E. Brown, *The Gospel According to John (i–xii)*. Anchor Bible 29. New York: Doubleday, 1966, 231–304 are dedicated to ch. 6.

HEARING AND SEEING

At the outset of this presentation, I noted the importance of learning how to read one another's classics, so I want to leave you with a Roman Catholic classic. The logic of our conference might have suggested that we compare John Calvin with Ignatius Loyola. Ignatius however left no commentary collection comparable in its scope and insight to Calvin's. Nevertheless, through the *Spiritual Exercises* he taught a new generation how to enter into the life-giving Word of God in Scripture through prayer and contemplation in a way that would provoke profound conversion of heart. Central to Ignatius's way of reading and praying Scripture is what he calls the 'composition of place'. This is a preliminary stage in the time of prayer in which the person praying is invited through the creative work of the imagination to see the place in the mind's eye where the story will unfold and the actors who take part in it.

It should be noted here that for contemplation or meditation about visible things, for example a contemplation on Christ our Lord (who is visible), the 'composition' will consist in seeing, through the gaze of the imagination, the material place where the object I want to contemplate is situated. By 'material place' I mean for example the temple or a mountain where Jesus Christ or our Lady is to be found – according to what I want to contemplate.[19]

---

19. Ignatius Loyola, *Spiritual Exercises* (Ex 47), cited from *The Spiritual Exercises of St Ignatius Loyola*, tr. Michael Ivens (Leominster: Gracewing, 2004). For a perceptive article on the function of the composition of place in Ignatian prayer, see Nicolas Standaert: 'The Composition of Place: Creating Space for an Encounter', *The Way*, 46/1 (January 2007), 7–20.

Ignatius's method of imaginative contemplation made a deep impression on Catholics of all levels, particularly perhaps on artists. As I was preparing this paper earlier in the summer, I read two recent books that are models of the biographer's art. The first was Bruce Gordon's biography of John Calvin.[20] The second was Andrew Graham-Dixon's *Caravaggio: A Life Sacred and Profane*.[21] Caravaggio was born less than a decade after the death of Calvin. It would be hard to think of two men who were less alike, but this conference has been about bringing unlikely conversation partners together, so let me try another one. In Roman Catholic and Orthodox tradition, iconic representation can be almost as powerful a commentary on the biblical text as the great written commentaries. The Reformation promoted literacy, for without it no one could read the Bible: it also had a suspicion of images and religious art.[22] The Catholic Counter Reform movement on the other hand gave a fresh impetus to painting and church decoration. One of the very great strengths of Graham-Dixon's portrayal of Caravaggio and his social world is his insistence on the importance of Charles Borromeo's church reform in Milan (1556-1584), in the spirit of Trent, for understanding the young Caravaggio. Ignatius's idea of the composition of place made profound impact on the artists of the Counter Reformation who applied its principles to give a new realism to biblical and religious paintings.

---

20. Bruce Gordon, *Calvin* (New Haven: Yale University Press, 2009).

21. Andrew Graham-Dixon, *Caravaggio: A Life Sacred and Profane* (London: Allen Lane, 2010).

22. For a study of one localised example, see Phyllis Mack Crew, *Calvinist Preaching and Iconoclasm in the Netherlands 1544–1569* (Cambridge: Cambridge University Press, 1978).

Caravaggio's religious paintings, such as the *Conversion of St Paul* in the Church of Santa Maria del Popolo (where Martin Luther lodged during his stay in Rome) or *The Supper at Emmaus* in the National Gallery, London, are well known. One of the most striking of them is his depiction of *The Incredulity of Thomas* (Potsdam, Germany). It is a scene familiar from the twentieth chapter of the Gospel of John. Caravaggio depicts the disciples in the picture as care-worn, poor, middle-aged or even elderly people with torn, frayed clothes and filthy fingernails. Yet it is into such a world of the poor and frayed that Jesus comes. It is to such as these that he returns as risen saviour, the only youthful figure in the painting, yet the one who promises new life. You can almost see a smile playing on his lips as he presses the dirty finger of Thomas into the wound in his side. As Caravaggio sees it, in this meeting of Thomas and Christ, humanity thrusts its dirty fingers into the very heart of God. Just as Calvin wrestled with the Word in writing, Carvaggio wrestled with it in paint. For both of them, it was a Word that brought a promise of new life and hope.

CHAPTER 5

The Spirituality of John Calvin and Ignatius Loyola: A Workshop[1]

Tom Wilson and Tom Layden

TOM WILSON

To explain why I am here, let me tell you a little story. Not surprisingly, it is about a Presbyterian Moderator who had just finished service on Sunday morning in a particular church. He had been invited by the minister of the church to lunch with his family afterwards. So while the minister and his wife went to the kitchen to prepare lunch, they left their young son in conversation with the Moderator. The boy asked the Moderator: 'how does a person become a Moderator?' The Moderator said, 'Well, you have to be very dedicated at school. You have to go to Sunday school every Sunday, learn all the lessons and become one of the best pupils. After that, you go to theological college, study hard and try to be one of the best students there. When you become a minister, you have to work hard and be one of the best ministers.' Just then, as the parents entered to call them to the table, they heard the boy say: 'Well, that does not seem too hard. Mum and Dad were wondering earlier just how on earth you became the Moderator!' When I got the brochure for the conference, I wondered: 'How did I become involved in doing this?' So let me begin at the beginning.

---

1. This presentation was delivered orally. The text was transcribed from the recording by the editor.

On 13 September 1999, I began to work through the *Spiritual Exercises* of St Ignatius of Loyola according to what is known as Annotation 19, or 'the exercises in daily life', rather than in the context of a thirty-day retreat. I was in the early stages of being a Presbyterian minister. It was not common then, and it is probably still not very common, for Presbyterian ministers to include the Exercises of St Ignatius in their spiritual formation. I had come to a place in my spiritual journey where I wanted a deeper connecting with God, to know God even more closely. I had a very solid Evangelical background in theology and practise in my earlier years, that had contributed to the work I was doing. I had worked largely in the area of social justice. For quite a number of years, I had worked with the probation service and in counselling so I was drawn to working with people who experienced difficulties in their background. I was interested when Stephen Williams mentioned Calvin's interest in social justice and that he had written over two hundred sermons on Deuteronomy.[2] I had a strong sense of calling to ordained ministry in the Presbyterian Church. I still felt also a longing for a deeper life of prayer. There was also incorporated into my background a significant amount of charismatic theology and practise.

I came into contact with Brian Grogan, a Jesuit who was then working in Belfast and has since returned to Dublin. I asked him one day over lunch: 'Could you tell me something about the *Exercises* of Ignatius?' The upshot was that I soon embarked on a journey through the Exercises over nine months with Brian as my spiritual director. It was a journey that was of incredible significance for me and it had an immense impact on my life,

---

2. See chapter 1 of this collection, Stephen N. Williams, 'Living in Union with Christ according to John Calvin'.

on my spiritual life and subsequently on my ministry. Some time after that Brian left Belfast and Tom Layden returned. We formed a very strong friendship that has continued over the years. Together, we have run courses on prayer, both in my church and in Union College. I have always found Tom to be very sensitive to where we are coming from in our tradition, and to be very good at building bridges. There were a number of things we were able to do together. As an outworking of that, I went and trained in spiritual direction and have been involved in that for a number of years.

What were some of the things in the *Exercises* that made an impact on me? First of all, they were Word-centred: in fact, they are saturated in the Bible. Second, they expressed and demonstrated a spirituality that was entirely dependent on the grace of God. Third, they emphasised the need for conversion, repentance and forgiveness. Finally, at their core, they pointed towards the importance of a continued personal relationship with Christ. If those aspects of spirituality were already familiar to me from my Presbyterian background, what was different about the *Exercises*? It was perhaps, not so much 'what was different', rather 'how was it different'. At the heart of the *Exercises*, there is something that enables us to engage with the reality of what we believe in such a way that we experience it as a lived reality in our lives. That aspect of the *Exercises* has become more widely known over the last thirty or forty years or so, and over the last decade in particular, among those who are not from a Catholic background.

Let me give you two quotations that speak about the significance of the *Exercises*. The first is from Dallas Willard, professor of philosophy at the University of Southern California and a leading Evangelical figure:

The *Spiritual Exercises* of Ignatius is one of the very few works produced by followers of Christ that reliably guides those who have seriously put their confidence in Christ unto a path where that which we Christians endlessly talk about becomes the reality of daily existence. This is because Ignatius guides the disciple into experience of the things we talk about. That reality stands out in the details of what is experienced.[3]

Willard also speaks positively about Calvin in his writings and, in particular, he draws attention to what Calvin has to say about self-denial, but here he is speaking positively about the *Exercises* and how they help people find the reality of what it is they are looking for, what they long for and why they sometimes seem to be frustrated because they cannot find what helps them to make the change. The other Evangelical witness is David Benner, professor of psychology and spirituality at the Psychological Studies Institute of Atlanta. 'Four centuries before the rise of modern psychology,' he says, 'Ignatius gave us the most psychologically grounded understanding of the Christian spiritual journey that has yet to be developed.'[4]

It seems to me that the Exercises have been constructed in a way that enables people to engage in a realistic manner with a process that will open them to the grace of God coming to them. I believe that is something inherent within the Exercises. David Lonsdale, a Jesuit writer, describes how, in the 1960s, Jesuit spirituality

---

3. Dallas Willard's comment on the value of the Ignatian Exercises is from his recommendation in the flyleaf of Larry Warner, *Journey with Jesus: Discovering the Spiritual Exercises of Saint Ignatius* (Nottingham: InterVarsity Press, 2010)

4. David Benner, *Desiring God's Will: Aligning Our Hearts with the Hearts of God*, (Nottingham: InterVarsity Press, 2005), 108.

took on new energy and found a new direction.[5] Shortly after Ignatius's death, key elements of his way of proceeding appear to have been lost. For example, the *Exercises* were normally given in the form of preached retreats. The perspective has changed now, and there is a return to Ignatius's own practice of giving the Exercises through individual meetings between the person who is making them and the one who is directing them. We have been coming more and more of late to recognise the importance of the spirituality of Calvin, but comparatively little has been written on this theme to match the body of literature on the Exercises.

TOM LAYDEN

Growing up in the west of Ireland, which of the two, Calvin or Loyola, did I hear of first? Actually I heard of Calvin first. We did the Reformation in fifth class. My mother's family, the McCarrons, were originally Church of Scotland. When I was in sixth class, I had to do the entrance examination for Clongowes College, run by the Jesuits. I was worried about the examination: if they asked me: 'Who was the founder of the Jesuits?' What was I to say? I asked my mother. She did not know either. She asked the parish priest who told me, the night before the examination, that Ignatius Loyola was the founder of the Jesuits. Later, as a University student, I worked with the Corrymeela programme in Armagh city. I found myself going regularly on a Sunday to Third Armagh Presbyterian Congregation, just to see what it was like. While there were differences, there were also many things I liked and felt at home with – especially the Scriptures and the singing. I became friendly with one of the elders and was impressed by the centrality of his faith in Jesus Christ.

---

5. David Lonsdale, *Eyes to See, Ears to Hear: An Introduction to Ignatian Spirituality* (London: Darton, Longman and Todd, 2000), 170.

Tom Wilson has asked me to say something about the similarities between Calvin and Ignatius and what I think they had in common. When I joined the Jesuits in 1979, I made the Spiritual Exercises during my first year. Two moments in the Exercises reminded me of my friend Ian, the elder in Armagh. The first was during the first week when Ignatius would have us pray about the reality of sin. That is certainly one thing Ignatius and Calvin have in common: they both take sin seriously. There can be a way of thinking about sin that is unhealthy, morbidly self-preoccupied or unhelpful. But sin is a reality in the world, and if we look away from it, we are just not living life as it really is. Calvin and Ignatius have a sense that we can only take sin seriously in the context of God's overarching mercy, made visible for us in Jesus Christ. In one of the Exercises, Ignatius would have us pray, imagining that we are kneeling or standing before Christ on the cross and asking ourselves: 'What have I done for Christ? What am I doing for Christ? What will I do for Christ?' This brought me back to my memory of my conversations with Ian, to his great sense that we are sinners, that the grace revealed to us in the death and resurrection of Jesus Christ sets us free and that we have to make a response to that grace. The second occasion was during the third week of the Exercises when we meditate on Jesus in his Passion. Ignatius would have us recall that Jesus goes to the cross out of love for me, a sinner. That was something very strong in what Ian had passed on to me, that Jesus dies personally for me as a sinner. So in my own story of discipleship, I found the two parts of my reality, Catholic and Presbyterian, dovetailing and reinforcing each other.

It seems to me that both Calvin and Ignatius want us to be focused on Jesus Christ. They would be disappointed if we focused on them instead. For me, one way of understanding Ignatius's spirituality is to see it as a key to reading the Scriptures, to reading how God had dealt with humankind: how God had created us, how the gift of freedom had been misused, how God has responded in the incarnation, ministry, death and resurrection of his son. Ignatius Loyola and John Calvin would not have us skim through the Scriptures, but would want us to see God's word as a message we must take seriously. They both have a strong sense of God's plan, leading up that great revelation of divine love in the Paschal Mystery of his son. Another theme I believe they have in common is a belief in the sovereignty of God. We are dependent on God; we are part of God's creation. If we put ourselves at the centre, if we lose our sense of creature-hood, then we've got it wrong. They also have a strong sense that God's love relates to every aspect of our lives, whether it is eating breakfast, whether it is giving a talk, whether it is travelling. I am accompanying Jesus Christ, or more accurately, Jesus Christ is accompanying me, in each of these moments. Both also put an emphasis on giving glory to God, a sense that the purpose of our being created is to give honour, praise and glory to God. In the world in which we live, it is very easy to become self-referential and self-focused.

Another emphasis they have in common, I believe, is their stress on community. There is no such thing as a private Christianity. Stephen Williams described Calvin's Geneva for us. One could say all sorts of things about it, both positive and negative, but Calvin was trying to establish a context in which the Christian life could be well lived. Maybe he was trying to be too protective: we would probably do it differently nowadays, but his basic aim was to create a community in which people would flourish in the way that God would have them flourish.

When Ignatius was setting up his religious order, he also gave guidelines for the members who were joining. It included many very practical things: for example there was as much emphasis on physical health as on spiritual health. Calvin and Loyola were both willing to challenge their communities. There was a high cost to be paid. Ignatius asked those joining his order: 'Are you willing to suffer insults, poverty, hardships with Christ?' If you are going to walk the way of Christ then you have to walk the way of the cross. They both put an emphasis on the cross. They are not promoting an easy Christianity. It is a demanding Gospel, but a demanding Gospel which, at the end of the day, is Good News for each of us in the depths of our heart, a Gospel that offers the word of freedom, offers the fullness of life. They both had a suspicion (and I think this also comes down to us in both our traditions) of those who would look for honour or prestige and too much comfort. Ignatius speaks of how you should be happy with the worst room in the house instead of looking for the best one. They would have us understand that the important thing is not the honours people give us, nor our comfort. The important thing is the relationship with God offered to us in the Lord's cross, in his death and in his resurrection. Early in the *Spiritual Exercises*, Ignatius would have us be moved to utter a great cry of wonder, that in the midst of all our backsliding and failure, God has remained faithful to us and in Christ, he is offering us the key to the fullness of life. I once said to John Dunlop, after I had been attending his church almost every week for a year, that I found there a sense of coming home. Our two traditions have much in common. Both Loyola and Calvin had a great love for the Church, the community of the disciples of Jesus Christ. That came out of their love of Christ and their desire that we would do whatever is possible to give praise, honour and glory to God and to fulfil the purpose of our creating. Working with Tom over the past ten years has given me an insight into how, as ministers together, the Spirit has been able to work through us, that work has produced fruit and today is another stage in that.

TOM WILSON

This is a workshop, so we want for a while to focus on one particular aspect of what seems to be coming from the spirituality of both John Calvin and Ignatius Loyola. It was a belief, based in Scripture and theology and on their own life experience, that it was possible for individuals to encounter God on a daily basis in lived experience. What we would like you to do now is move into groups of three. Here is the scenario: imagine you are sitting in a coffee shop. You are in your own space but you are not pressed for time. Someone comes over to you: you may recognise them vaguely but they probably have a better idea of who you are. They open the conversation by saying: 'I believe in Jesus Christ, I attend church regularly, I worship with other believers, I read the Bible and I pray. I find a text in Proverbs 9:10, for example, where it says that "the knowledge of the Holy One is understanding" and I know that Jesus said "now this is eternal life to know you the only true God and Jesus Christ whom you have sent" (Jn 17:3). I know as well that the Apostle Paul said "I consider everything a loss compared with the surpassing greatness of knowing Jesus Christ my Lord" (Phil 3:8).' Then they ask, 'Can you tell me how I can really know God?' This is not someone who needs an initial introduction to Christ. It is someone who is keen, who is involved in practise and who sees the Bible as saying, 'It is possible for me to know God'. There is your conversation. In a coffee shop you would have about thirty seconds before you reply: you have already had that long now.

What we are asking you to do is to take turns, two minutes each, answering the question: 'How is it possible for me to know God?'

AFTER TEN MINUTES OF WORK IN SMALL GROUPS

Thanks very much for entering into the spirit of that discussion. You have been discussing how it is possible to know God. That is a very central aspect to the spirituality of the two people we have been considering. A commentary on John's Gospel says that this knowing is not an intellectual assent. The Hebrew notion of knowing encompasses experience and intimacy. For Christians, that means obedience and love for God. Dallas Willard, the philosopher, distinguishes between knowledge by description and knowledge by acquaintance. Only the latter is an interactive relationship. That is what we see in Calvin and Loyola. Calvin spoke of piety as the worship of God that was a deep personal experience:

> By means of the Holy Spirit, we become partakers of the divine nature, so as in a moment to feel its quickening energy within us ... For the pious soul has the best view of God and may almost be said to handle him, for it feels that it is quickened, enlightened, saved, justified, and sanctified by him (*Institutes*, I.xiii.13).

The believer feels the majesty of God, the divinity of God, the actions of God, God's fatherhood and God's presence. There is also that sentence that opens the *Institutes* where Calvin says there is no deep knowledge of God without a deep knowing of self or any knowing of self without a deep knowing of God. Ignatius too has this unshakeable belief, that he held on to as a rock in all storms, that God can be encountered in our experience. God comes directly to men and women and they will recognise God's presence if they open their heart to him. The purpose of the Exercises is to help people to experience God directly and powerfully. Knowing God is of critical importance for us individually and for the Church. The knowing of God has been consigned to something that is no longer regarded as 'knowledge' in the academy. That has had an incredible influence on all of us. What is it we are doing when we are proclaiming the Christian message? Is it a proclamation of sincerely held belief or is it a proclamation of knowledge on which all of humanity can base their lives and their existence?

Back in 1983, Karl Rahner wrote a sentence that has been much quoted since: 'the Christian of the future will be a mystic or he or she will not exist at all'.[6] He was talking about the importance of knowing God in our experience. We can have caricatures of what it means to know God. Just to give you another opportunity to do something for yourselves, I want to focus on some questions from the 'examination of consciousness' in the *Exercises*. Ignatius suggests that even if your time is so squeezed on any particular day, that you do not have time for much else by way of prayer, never to omit this prayer form. It is a way of reflecting on our experience. It is not intended to be introspective, but it is to help me notice where God is present with me. Where have I turned towards God's presence? Where have I turned away from it? We will give you another few minutes to work on this. For about four or five minutes, reflect quietly on these initial questions: 'When in the past twenty-four hours did I turn towards God?' You might ask yourself, for instance, 'Can I think of an occasion, of a moment of interaction, of something

---

6. Karl Rahner, 'The Spirituality of the Church of the Future', *Theological Investigations 20* (New York: Crossroads, 1981), 143–53.

that happened when I turned towards or when I realised I was turning towards God, deepening my acquaintance with God?' The second question is: 'When did I turn away from God?' You might recognise turning towards God as peace, so did you recognise that the peace of God was with you? As you reflect, did you notice that you were disturbed, or as you now think of it, were you actually turning away from God? These are questions from the Ignatian examen, so just take a few minutes with them.

TOM LAYDEN
When Tom and I were involved in giving courses and chatting with people towards the end of a session, I would sometimes hear them say something like this. For Presbyterians, it might be: 'We know the Scriptures well, some parts of it we know particularly well, but maybe what we really need is help to pray the Scriptures, to hear the Scriptures as a word addressed to me in the concrete circumstances of my life.' Catholics on the other hand might say: 'We learned many prayers down through the years but did we really learn to pray? Did we really learn to wait in silence and openness to hear what God is saying to us?' These are just two distillations of currents that came to us. What we have been exploring in this workshop is how Calvin and Ignatius point us towards knowing God, knowing Jesus Christ. There is a kind of knowledge that is 'knowing about'. For example, I may know the causes of the First World War, I may know the main battles, I may even know the consequences of the First World War. But I was not there. I did not take part in it. 'Knowing about' can be abstract. But if I talked to someone who had taken part in the war (and I did once), then the effect is very different. When we talk about our knowledge of God and Jesus Christ, it is not knowledge from theory. There is a very

important science of theology when we reflect upon faith but at heart, our knowledge of God and Jesus Christ is a personal knowledge and in praying the Scriptures, it is to be led to that personal knowledge of Jesus Christ.

Earlier I spoke about how, as I was moving from primary school to secondary school, I felt inadequate. There is a woundedness in all of us and that woundedness means that at times we feel inadequate. At other times, we lose the run of ourselves and we feel super-adequate in a way that is unrealistic. I think both Ignatius and Calvin want us to know ourselves as we are – people who are dependent on God, people who are vulnerable, but people who God loves. It is in our personal sense of God's love that we have a sense of who we really are. There is a lovely line from the Letter to the Romans (8:28) where Paul says: 'to those who love God, who are called according to his plan, everything works to the good.' Those words can only become real in my life when I know Jesus Christ personally, when I have spent time with him in personal prayer, when I have brought to him my own woundedness, as I have experienced it in my life in different ways and at different times, when I bring to him the times I have overestimated myself and got it wrong. Let him speak a word to me through the Scripture heard in the actual reality of my life.

Back in the mid-1980s, I was teaching religion to a group of fifteen year olds. I was dreadfully unsuccessful! The course had an emphasis on why we believe in God. What I ended up saying to them was, 'I can speak about knowing God because of two things.' The two things were the Scriptures and the experiences of my own life. If we dally for a while with the writings of John Calvin and Ignatius Loyola, we will realise how, despite their differences, they lead us to a sense of a God showing his love to us through the Risen Son who has died for us, who is risen for us and who is with us in our lives as we lead them day by day.

Tom and I had a series of meetings as we were planning today's session. At one of them we asked ourselves: 'What do we hope the people will leave the room with today?' We did not want to prejudge. The Holy Spirit might have had other plans and we wanted to respect your freedom, but the hope we articulated was that as you left, you might have a sense that our knowledge of God is not something impersonal and academic but that our knowledge of God is something heartfelt, personal and experiential, something that is real in my life as I live it today, whether things are going well or whether there is a struggle. But that we will leave to yourselves and the Holy Spirit.

CHAPTER 6

Calvin and the Holy Spirit

Stafford Carson

I grew up in a Pentecostal church in the days before the charismatic movement really took off. A common mantra heard in those circles at that time was that the Holy Spirit was the forgotten member of the Trinity. The understanding was that most Churches talked about God the Father and Jesus Christ the Son, but that in the majority of Churches there was little reference to the Holy Spirit. Apparently the work and ministry of the Holy Spirit was overlooked by mainstream Christianity in general and by Evangelicalism in particular. Pentecostal churches, by giving a more central role to the doctrine of the Holy Spirit in their preaching and worship, were trying to redress the imbalance. It was from its beginnings in the Azusa Street Revival in the early years of the twentieth century that there was a new interest in the work and ministry of the Holy Spirit. The Welsh evangelist, George Jeffreys, came to Ireland in 1915 and, as a result of his ministry, Elim Pentecostal churches were planted, firstly in Monaghan, and then in a number of towns and villages across the North of Ireland.

The good people who attended these meetings were aware of a reality and an enthusiasm that they had not seen elsewhere. They rejoiced in a new sense of God's presence in their worship. Then, in the 1960s, people in the mainline denominations developed an interest in the gifts and ministry of the Holy

Spirit, many of them claiming to have a new experience of the Holy Spirit and to have known the Spirit's work in their lives in new and wonderful ways. I remember as a teenager attending meetings in Belfast where Presbyterians and Anglicans were worshipping together with their Pentecostal brothers and sisters and where the so-called revelatory gifts of the Spirit were in evidence.

Things have moved on at a fast pace since then. Today, charismatic churches and fellowships dominate the ecclesiastical landscape, and the growth of the Church in Africa and Asia and South America is characterised by all the features we associate with charismatic churches. In his important book on world Christianity, Philip Jenkins points out how that Christianity will continue to expand in the global south, but the question that remains unanswered is whether it will be Catholic Christianity or charismatic Christianity.[1] We need to recognise that we now live in a world where many Christians rejoice in the work and ministry of the Holy Spirit.

When I came to an understanding of Reformed theology, and began reading some of the older Reformed writers, I discovered that the original claim about the Holy Spirit being the forgotten member of the Trinity in non-Pentecostal and Reformed churches was largely untrue. It may have been true that traditional Reformed worship lacked the energy and the vitality (and the excesses!) of Pentecostal or charismatic worship, but a careful look at the theology of the Reformation revealed a very clear and profound appreciation for the work and ministry of the Holy Spirit. That understanding of the person and work of the Spirit is seen very clearly in the thinking and

---

1. Philip Jenkins, *The Next Christendom: The Coming of Global Christianity* (Oxford: Oxford University Press, 2007).

theology of John Calvin. I would go further and say that even now the doctrine of the Holy Spirit that is believed and taught in Reformed churches is richer and deeper than that which is found among those who profess to emphasise the importance of the Spirit's work and ministry.

Those who think that the Holy Spirit has only been discovered in the twentieth century are guilty, at best, of historical short-sightedness, and, at worst, of the heresy of modernity. They have forgotten that it was with good reason that John Calvin was described as 'the theologian of the Holy Spirit'. While his work has been recognised, the Spirit remains to many Christians an anonymous, faceless aspect of the divine being. Perhaps it would be better to say that the Holy Spirit is the 'unknown' rather than the 'forgotten' person of the Trinity. That is why a return to the theology of John Calvin can be so helpful and necessary for the Church today.

While John Calvin may be best known for his doctrine of predestination and election – although Augustine and Luther wrote more than he did about that subject – he was even more committed to the theology of the Holy Spirit. Abraham Kuyper (1837-1920), who was an outstanding churchman and politician in the Netherlands, becoming its prime minister, credited Calvin with being one of the greatest commentators on the Holy Spirit.

The doctrine of the work of the Holy Spirit is a gift from John Calvin to the Church of Christ. He did not, of course, invent it. The whole of it lay spread out on the pages of Scripture with a clearness and fullness of utterance which one would think would secure that even he who ran should read it; and doubtless he who ran did read it, and it has fed the soul of the true believer in all ages.[2]

---

2. Abraham Kuyper, *The Work Of The Holy Spirit*, trans. Henri de Vries (New York: Funck and Wagnalls, 1900).

Kuyper added, 'Luther rose to proclaim justification by faith, and Calvin to set forth with his marvellous balance the whole doctrine of the work of the Spirit in applying salvation to the soul.' I believe that the theology of John Calvin has a contemporary relevance for Christians and for the Church today. I wish in this paper to point out a number of areas where we need to listen to Calvin again, and how, by listening to what he said and wrote, some of our current confusion and ignorance with regard to the Holy Spirit can be clarified and we can come to an enriched understanding of our faith. I will look at the following areas: Calvin's understanding of the work and ministry of the Holy Spirit in salvation, in the doctrine of assurance, in our understanding of Scripture, and finally with regard to the sacraments.

The work of the Spirit in salvation

The title given to Book 3 of Calvin's *Institutes of the Christian Religion* is this: 'The way in which we receive the grace of Christ: what benefits come to us from it, and what effects follow.' In the latter half of Book 2 of the *Institutes*, Calvin has dealt with the finished work of Christ, the once-for-all accomplishment of salvation. Now, in Book 3, he understands himself to be concerned with the application or the personal appropriation of salvation. It is about 'the grace of Christ', its 'benefits' and 'consequent effects', and the way, or the mode, or the manner, in which believers receive this grace, the manner in which this salvation is appropriated.

With that concern restated in the opening words of Book 3, the very next sentence reads like this:

> First, we must understand that as long as Christ remains outside of us, and we are separated from him, all that he has suffered and done for the salvation of the human race remains useless and of no value to us (III.i.1).

It is difficult to exaggerate the importance of that sentence for Calvin's doctrine of salvation as a whole. Positioned as it is at the opening of Book 3, it expresses what is most fundamental for him, the consideration that underlies all other considerations within the application of redemption. This most deeply decisive consideration, put negatively here, is that Christ not remain 'outside us', that we are not to be 'separated from him'. Or if we are to express it positively, as Calvin presently does, that 'we grow into one body with him'.[3]

It is interesting and noteworthy that as his point of departure for all that he will say in Book 3, he begins by bringing into view and highlighting the union that exists between Christ and believers. So central and pivotal is this union for the application of redemption that, again expressing it negatively, he can even say that without it the saving work of Christ 'remains useless and of no value'. This union, he immediately goes on to make clear, is 'obtained by faith', as it does not exist apart from, or prior to, faith but is given with faith and is inseparable from faith. This mention of faith, and the key role accorded to it, prompts Calvin, still within this opening section, to touch on what would become a central question in subsequent discussions about the *ordo salutis*, or the order of salvation. That question was about the origin of faith, and eventually gave rise in Reformed

---

3. Richard B. Gaffin Jr, 'Justification and Union with Christ', *Theological Guide to Calvin's Institutes*, eds. David W. Hall and Peter A. Lillback (Phillipsburg, NJ: P&R, 2008).

theology to the doctrine of regeneration in the narrower sense. We observe, says Calvin, 'that not all indiscriminately embrace that communion with Christ which is offered through the Gospel'.

Why is that? Why is it that some people respond in faith to the Gospel and others do not? It is not because of some differentiating factor on our side. The answer is not to be found by looking into ourselves or contemplating the mystery of human freedom and human willing. Rather, consistent with his uniform teaching elsewhere about the total inability of the human will because of sin, we must, says Calvin, 'climb higher' and consider 'the secret energy of the Spirit'. When he writes like that, talking about the secret energy of the Spirit, he sounds almost charismatic! For Calvin faith is Spirit-worked, sovereignly and efficaciously. It is dependent on the energy and dynamic work of the Holy Spirit. Union with Christ, then, is forged by the Spirit's working faith in us, a faith that puts on Christ, as he quotes Galatians 3:27: 'For all of you who were baptised into Christ have clothed yourselves with Christ.' It is a faith that embraces Christ as he is offered in the Gospel. Faith is the bond of that union seen from our side. 'To sum up,' he says, 'the Holy Spirit is the bond by which Christ effectually unites us to himself.' Subsequently, Calvin will categorise this union as both 'spiritual' and 'mystical'.

This, at its core, is Calvin's *ordo salutis*: union with Christ by Spirit-worked faith. From that overall vantage point at the beginning of Book 3, we come to understand that justification is by faith alone because union with Christ is by faith alone, and it is that union which brings with it justification. This union is one of the Gospel's greatest mysteries. One commentator points out that there at least seven instances in the Institutes where Calvin uses the Latin words *arcanus* or *incomprehensibilis* to describe union with Christ. This doctrine of union with Christ shapes Calvin's understanding of regeneration, faith, justification, sanctification, assurance, election and the Church. He could scarcely speak of any doctrine apart from union and communion with Christ.

Union and communion with Christ is realised only through Spirit-worked faith. It is actual union and communion, not because believers participate in the essence of Christ's nature, but because the Spirit unites believers so intimately to Christ that they become flesh of his flesh and bone of his bone. Indeed, the spiritual union with Christ that the Holy Spirit forges within us is even closer than physical union. Calvin puts it this way:

> Let us know the unity that we have with the Lord Jesus Christ; to wit, that he wills to have a common life with us, and that what he has should be ours; nay, that he even wishes to dwell in us, not in imagination, but in effect; not in earthly fashion, but spiritually; and that whatever may befall, he so labours by the virtue of his Holy Spirit that we are united with him more closely than are the limbs with the body.[4]

The culmination of this complete and entire union with Christ in both body and soul will be fully realised in our resurrection from the dead on the judgement day.

Thus Christ and the Holy Spirit work together for our salvation. Though distinct, they are inseparable. Calvin moves easily from saying 'The Spirit dwelling in us' to 'Christ dwelling

---

4. 'Sermon on the Resurrection', online version accessed at http://www.monergism.com/thethreshold/sdg/calvin/calvin_36sermons.html#sermon11 (accessed 30 August, 2011).

in us' (*Institutes*, III.ii.39). Jesus Christ is the unique bearer and bestower of the Spirit. Every action of the Spirit is, in essence, the action of Christ. The Spirit bestows nothing on us of a saving nature but through the Spirit. That is clear from his title of chapter 1 of Book 3: 'The things spoken concerning Christ profit us by the secret working of the Spirit. Christ works salvation through the Spirit, and the Holy Spirit works salvation for Christ in sinners' hearts.' Calvin quotes I Peter 1:2: we 'have been chosen according to the foreknowledge of God the Father, through the sanctifying work of the Holy Spirit, for obedience to Jesus Christ and sprinkling by his blood'. He says, 'By these words he explains that, in order that the shedding of his sacred blood may not be nullified, our souls are cleansed by the secret watering of the Spirit' (III.i.1).[5] The Holy Spirit is thus the bond by which Christ effectually unites us to himself.

For Calvin, the Holy Spirit is the root and the seed of heavenly life within us. That is why, he says, when the prophets and apostles look forward to the advancement of Christ's kingdom and the fact that God will make disciples of those who were previously destitute and empty of heavenly doctrine, they describe it as a richer outpouring of the Holy Spirit. The events of Pentecost, when the gospel breaks out from the small group of disciples gathered in the Upper Room and people from every nation hear the praises of God in their own language, happen as a direct result of the fulfilment of Joel's prophesy where God promises: 'I will pour out my Spirit upon all flesh' (Joel 2:28). It is the Spirit who separates us from the world and gathers us unto the hope of the eternal inheritance.

---

5. Unless otherwise stated, subsequent references in text are to the *Institutes*.

In discussing the whole question of salvation, Calvin says it is useful to note what titles are applied to the Holy Spirit in Scripture. These titles help us to understand the importance of the role of the Spirit in our salvation. The Spirit is called the Spirit of adoption because it witnesses to us of the way God the Father has embraced us in his Son, Jesus Christ, in order to become a father to us. And so when we come to God in prayer, we come without fear, because it is the Spirit who supplies us with the very words that we may use. We may cry 'Abba, Father' because of the work and ministry of the Spirit. The Spirit is also called the seal and guarantee of our inheritance. In our pilgrimage through this world, the Spirit assures us that our salvation is safe in God's unfailing care. Calvin is eager to refer to the Spirit by the Bible's own words: the Spirit is water and the spring; the Spirit is oil and fire. By his secret watering, the Spirit makes us fruitful, enabling us to bring forth the fruits of righteousness in our lives. The image of water is also appropriate because of the Spirit's power to cleanse and purify us: as fire, the Spirit enflames our hearts with the love of God and with zealous devotion for Christ:

> For by the inspiration of his power he so breathes divine life into us that we are no longer actuated by ourselves, but are ruled by his action and prompting. Accordingly, whatever good things are in us are the fruits of his grace; and without him our gifts are darkness of mind and perversity of heart (III.i.3).

With regard to the application of redemption, the Spirit has an enormous role, according to Calvin. As personal comforter, seal, and earnest, the Holy Spirit assures the believer of his adoption. Commenting on Romans 8:16, Calvin says:

> The Spirit of God gives us such a testimony that when he is our guide and teacher our spirit is made sure of the adoption of God; for our mind of itself, without the preceding testimony of the Spirit, could not convey to us this assurance.[6]

So Calvin reasons along these lines: (1) the purpose of election embraces salvation; (2) the elect are not chosen for anything in themselves, but only in Christ; (3) since the elect are in Christ, the assurance of their election and salvation can never be found in themselves, or even in the Father apart from Christ; (4) rather, their assurance is to be found in Christ. So it follows that communion with him is vital.

THE SPIRIT'S ROLE WITH REGARD TO ASSURANCE

When it comes to the doctrine of assurance of salvation, and how believers may know that they are truly united to Christ, Calvin's answer again centres on the work of the Holy Spirit. It is the Holy Spirit who applies Christ and his benefits to the hearts and lives of guilty, elect sinners, assuring them that Christ belongs to them and they to him. The Holy Spirit especially confirms within them the reliability of God's promises in Christ. Personal assurance, then, is never divorced from the election of God the Father, the redemption of the Son, the application of the Spirit, and the instrumental means of saving faith.

The Holy Spirit's work underlies all assurance of salvation, without detracting from the role of Christ, for as the Spirit of

---

6. John Calvin, *Commentary on Romans* 8:16.

Christ he assures the believer by leading him to Christ and his benefits, and by bringing those benefits to fruition in the believer (III.ii.34). The unity of Christ and the Spirit has sweeping implications for the doctrine of assurance. Some recent scholars have minimised Calvin's emphasis on the necessity of the Spirit's work in assuring a believer of God's promises. The ground of assurance supposedly is God's promises, in Christ and/or in the Word of God, whereas the cause of assurance is the Spirit who works in the heart. Others have argued that this distinction is too simplistic, since the Spirit always works as the Spirit of Christ. Hence the objective and subjective elements in assurance cannot be so readily separated. Objective salvation in Christ is bound to subjective sealing by the Spirit. So it is Christ, in and through his Spirit, who is the ground of our faith. For Calvin, a believer's objective reliance upon God's promises as the primary ground for assurance must be subjectively sealed by the Holy Spirit for true assurance. The unbeliever or reprobate may claim God's promises without experiencing the feeling or consciousness of those promises. The Spirit often works in the reprobate, but in an inferior manner. They may be momentarily illumined so that they seem to have a beginning of faith; nevertheless, Calvin says that they 'never receive anything but a confused awareness of grace' (III.ii.11).

On the other hand, the elect are regenerated with incorruptible seed (III.ii.41). They receive subjective benefits that the reprobate will never taste. They alone receive the promises of God as truth in the inward parts. They alone receive the testimony that can be called 'the enlightening of the Spirit'. They alone receive experiential, intuitive knowledge of God as he offers himself to them in Christ (I.iv.1; II.vi.4,19). Calvin says that the elect alone come to be 'ravished and wholly kindled to love God; [they] are borne up to heaven itself [and] admitted to the most hidden treasures of God' (III.ii.41) and again 'the Spirit, strictly speaking, seals forgiveness of sins in the elect alone, so that they apply it by special faith to their own use' (III.ii.11).

The elect alone come to know special faith and a special inward testimony. When distinguishing the elect from the reprobate, Calvin speaks more about what the Spirit does in us than what Christ does for us, because it is here that the line of demarcation is sharper. He speaks much of inward experience, of feeling, of enlightenment, of perception, and even of 'violent emotion'. This may sound surprising to some of us within the Reformed family. Calvin may even sound a bit too charismatic or Pentecostal for our liking, but I think we need to recognise the intensely experiential nature of Calvin's doctrine of faith and assurance. He is aware of the dangers of excessive introspection, but he also recognises that the promises of God are only efficient when they are brought by the Spirit within the scope, experience and obedience of faith (III.i.1).

To summarise Calvin's position on the believer's assurance of faith, it is a case of all three members of the Trinity being involved. The election of the Father, the work of Christ, and the application of the Holy Spirit are all complementary. Christ is an overwhelming, foundational and primary source of assurance for the believer precisely because of the Spirit's application of Christ and his benefits to him as one elected by the Father. No one can ever be assured of Christ without the Spirit (III.ii.35). The Holy Spirit reveals to the believer through his Word that God is a well-disposed Father, and enables him to embrace Christ's promises by faith and with assurance.

THE ROLE OF THE HOLY SPIRIT IN OUR UNDERSTANDING OF SCRIPTURE

Another area which continues to be relevant in the contemporary Church is the relationship between Scripture and the Holy Spirit. Calvin's understanding of the Holy Spirit was far different from how many Christians use that phrase today. He believed in an inextricable connection between Scripture and the Spirit, i.e. that the Spirit, the third person of the Trinity, did not contradict or embellish the Bible. Nonetheless, he insisted, Scripture could be understood only by a Christian whose mind and heart had been subdued by the Spirit, in accordance with Scripture. Calvin deals with those whom he calls fanatics who separate the Spirit of God from the Word of God, and elevate the former in their experience over the latter. He writes in Book 1 of the *Institutes*:

> I would like to know from them what this spirit is by whose inspiration they are borne up so high that they dare despise the Scriptural doctrine as childish and mean ... by a heinous sacrilege these rascals tear apart those things which (cf. Isaiah 59:21) joined together (I.ix.1).

He goes on: 'we ought zealously to apply ourselves both to read and to hearken to the Scripture if indeed we want to receive any gain and benefit from the Spirit of God.' (I.ix.2). Later, he says:

> ... the Holy Spirit so inheres in his truth, which he expresses in Scripture, that only when its proper reverence and dignity are given to the Word does the Holy Spirit show forth his power ... By a kind of mutual bond the Lord has joined together the certainty of his Word and of his Spirit so that

117

the perfect religion of the Word may abide in our minds when the Spirit, who causes us to contemplate God's grace, shines (I.ix.3).

So Calvin argues in this section that the Spirit without the Word is a delusion, and the Word without the Spirit is dead: Word and Spirit ever belong together and must never be separated. The Holy Spirit speaking in Holy Scripture is the believer's final and ultimate authority in all matters of belief and behaviour. But the inner witness of the Holy Spirit, working by and with the Word in his heart, Calvin argued, confirms to the believer that the Bible is God's Word. That is to say, the Christian's confidence in Holy Scripture as the Word of God is produced by the Holy Spirit who graciously bears witness in the believer's heart at regeneration to the truthfulness of God's Word being proclaimed to him. Calvin writes that the

credibility of doctrine is not established until we are persuaded beyond doubt that God is its Author. Thus the highest proof of Scripture derives in general form from the fact that God in person speaks in it.

He continues:

If we desire to provide in the best way for our consciences - that they may not be perpetually beset by the instability of doubt or vacillation, and that they may not also boggle at the smaller quibbles - we ought to seek our conviction in a higher place than human reason, judgments, or conjectures, that is, in the secret testimony of the Spirit (I.vii.4).

Calvin said it was pointless (the word he used was 'backward') to attempt to prove Scripture's authority through disputation. He forsook what he called 'dexterity or eloquence' even though he believed that the 'clamorous voices' of sceptics could be easily silenced. His reasoning was that even with superior debating ability, until God 'imprinted on their heart that certainty that piety requires' unbelievers would 'stand by opinion alone'. Calvin argued that

> ... the testimony of the Spirit is more excellent than all reason. For as God alone is a fit witness of himself in his Word, so also the Word will not find acceptance in men's hearts before it is sealed by the inward testimony of the Spirit. The same Spirit therefore who has spoken through the mouths of the prophets must penetrate into our hearts to persuade us that they faithfully proclaimed what had been divinely commanded (I.vii.4).

He believed that it was not

> ... right to subject (Scripture) to proof and reasoning. And the certainty it deserves with us, it attains by the testimony of the Spirit. For even if it wins reverence for itself by its own majesty, it seriously affects us only when it is sealed upon our hearts through the Spirit. Therefore illumined by his power, we believe neither by our own or by anyone else's judgement that Scripture is from God; but above human judgement we affirm with utter certainty (just as if we were gazing upon the majesty of God himself) that it has flowed to us from the very mouth of God by the ministry of men (I.vii.5).

In short, Calvin's view relates the Spirit's testimonial work directly to the authority of the Word of God and not to its proofs. Robert Reymond argues that this is different from B.B. Warfield's understanding of Calvin. He says that Warfield understood Book 1, chapter viii of the *Institutes* as setting forth a list of evidentiary proofs by which the witnessing Spirit leads us to conclude that the Bible is divine. So he takes up these proofs into a 'probability argument' and makes them become the direct ground of our faith in Scripture. So Warfield relates the Spirit's testimony directly to these characteristics of Scripture as proofs and not to the divine authorship of Scripture.

The data that Calvin presents in I.viii to establish the credibility of the Bible is almost entirely drawn from the Scripture itself. He writes about 'the very heavenly majesty', the 'beautiful agreement of all the parts', the 'incontestable miracles', and the 'confirmed prophecy of the Old Testament'. He also mentions evidences not drawn directly from Scripture, such as the indestructibility of Scripture throughout the ages, its wide acceptance by the nations, and martyrs willing to die for it. But these are by no means the primary thrust of the chapter. It is the Holy Spirit who illumines the human mind, and brings conviction to it, directly by means of the Word of God, with the proofs being 'secondary aids to our feebleness'. Here is how he puts it in *Institutes* I.viii.13:

There are other reasons (than the ones mentioned in 1.viii) neither few nor weak, for which the dignity and majesty of Scripture are not only affirmed in godly hearts, but brilliantly vindicated against the wiles of its disparagers; yet of themselves, these are not strong enough to provide firm faith, until our Heavenly father, revealing his mystery there, lifts reverence for Scripture beyond the realm of controversy. Therefore Scripture will ultimately suffice for a saving knowledge of God only when its certainty is founded upon the inward persuasion of the Holy Spirit.

In short, Calvin's view relates the Spirit's testimonial work directly to the authority of the Word of God and not to its proofs. Here is how Louis Berkhof explains it:

The testimony of the Holy Spirit is simply the work of the Holy Spirit in the heart of the sinner by which he removes the blindness of sin, so that the erstwhile blind man who had no eyes for the sublime character of the Word of God, now clearly sees and appreciates the marks of its divine nature, and receives immediate certainty respecting the divine origin of Scripture. The testimony of the Holy Spirit is therefore ... not so much the final ground of faith, but rather the means of faith. The final ground of faith is Scripture only, or better still, the authority of God which is impressed upon the believer in the testimony of Scripture ... But the testimony of the Holy Spirit is the moving cause of faith. We believe Scripture, not because of, but through the testimony of the Holy Spirit.[7]

So Calvin understood that we come to receive the Scriptures as the Word of God that has authority through the work and testimony of the Holy Spirit.

---

7. Louis Berkhof, *Systematic Theology* (Grand Rapids: Eerdmanns 1996), 185.

THE ROLE OF THE SPIRIT IN THE SACRAMENTS

The role of the Holy Spirit is vital in understanding the sacraments, and especially the Lord's Supper. Only by appreciating fully the work of the Spirit can we avoid falling into the mistakes that have dogged both Catholic and evangelical misunderstandings of the Supper. I am very grateful to my friend and colleague Sinclair Ferguson for the way in which he describes this in his excellent book on the Holy Spirit.[8] It is not by the Church's administration, or merely by the activity of our memories that we enjoy communion with Christ. It is through the Spirit that we are brought into communion with the crucified, risen and exalted Christ. Christ is not localised in the bread and wine (as Catholic theology teaches): nor is he absent from the Supper so that our highest activity is remembering him (which is the memorialist view). Rather, Christ is known through the elements by the Spirit. There is a genuine communion with Christ in the Supper. Just as in the preaching of the Word he is present, not in the Bible locally, or by believing, but by the ministry of the Spirit. So he is also present in the Supper, not in the bread and wine, but by the power of the Spirit. The body and blood of Christ are not enclosed in the elements, since Christ is at the right hand of the Father. But by the power of the Spirit we are brought into his presence and he stands among us. I think that it is in this context that we should understand Revelation 3:20: 'behold I stand at the door and knock; if any man hear my voice and open the door, I will come in to him, and will sup with him, and he with me'. John, in the Spirit on the Lord's Day (cf. Rev 1:10), believed that this is the kind of fellowship that the Church might enjoy with her Saviour.

---

8. Sinclair B. Ferguson, *The Holy Spirit, Contours of Christian Theology Series* (Nottingham: InterVarsity Press, 1997).

No theologian has sought to understand this presence of Christ by his Spirit in the sacrament more thoroughly than Calvin. And yet, even in his strongest expressions of the meaning of the Supper, an admission of mystery remains:

> Even though it seems unbelievable that Christ's flesh, separated from us by such distance, penetrates to us, so that it becomes our food, let us remember how far the secret power of the Holy Spirit towers above all our senses, and how foolish it is to measure his immeasurableness by our measure. What, then, our mind does not comprehend, let faith conceive: that the Spirit truly unites things separated in space. Now, that sacred partaking of his flesh and blood, by which Christ pours his life into us, as if it penetrated into our bones and marrow, he also testifies and seals in the Supper – not by presenting a vain and empty sign, but by manifesting there the effectiveness of his Spirit to fulfil what he promises. And truly he offers and shows the reality there signified to all that sit at that spiritual banquet, although it is received with benefit by believers alone, who accept such great generosity with true faith and gratefulness of heart (IV.xvii.10).

Such thinking permeates Calvin's teaching. Christ comes to his people in the very body in which he was incarnate, crucified, buried, resurrected, ascended and is now glorified. Life is thus 'infused into us from the substance of his flesh' (IV.xvii.4). Calvin's language has evoked radically different reactions within the Reformed family. Charles Hodge, R.L. Dabney and William Cunningham all reacted negatively to his teaching in this area. They questioned it as seriously mistaken or simply incomprehensible, while others have greeted it as his deepest sacramental insight. There is no doubt that Calvin's language is far more realistic than much evangelical teaching on the Lord's Supper has been accustomed to be and, as a result, his exposition is thought to be excessively material. But, as Sinclair Ferguson says, the same could surely be said of the language of John 6:51-58, or for that matter, I Corinthians 10:16. If we are uncomfortable with Calvin's language, then our discomfort may mask a discomfort with the language of Scripture itself.

What is often overlooked in this discussion is the role and power which Calvin attributes to the Holy Spirit. Fundamental to his thinking about the Lord's Supper is the outworking of the correlation between Christ ascending and the Spirit descending. The Spirit descends in order to raise us up into fellowship with Christ. Similarly in the Supper, the Spirit comes, as it were, to close the gap between Christ in heaven and the believer on earth, and to give communion with the exalted Saviour. Calvin is asking another question: with what Christ does the believer commune at the table? His answer is: Christ clothed in the humanity in which he suffered, died and was buried, rose again, and is now ascended in glory. There is no other Christ than the enfleshed Word. In the Supper, we commune with the person of Christ in the mystery of the hypostatic union. We do so spiritually, through the power of the Holy Spirit.

Calvin does not need to be interpreted as saying more than this, and we should not say less than this, otherwise we deny the reality of the fellowship of which the New Testament speaks. Or we may risk denying the continuing reality of the humanity of the glorified Christ. Once we take seriously the truth of the bodily resurrection and ascension of Christ, Calvin's theology of the sacrament becomes less puzzling, although, as he admits himself, the truth it represents remains mysterious. But the mystery is no greater than it is with other aspects of the Spirit's work.

What then is the role of the Spirit in the Lord's Supper? It can be described in the words of John 16:14. The Spirit will take from what is Christ's and make it known to his disciples, he does this fundamentally through apostolic revelation. Nothing is revealed in the Supper that is not already made known in the Scriptures, but in the Supper there is visual representation and a simple and specific focus on the broken body and poured-out blood of Christ. This takes us to the heart of the matter and to the centre of the Spirit's ministry: it is to illumine the person and work of Christ. No new revelation is given. No other Christ is made known. We do not get a different or a better Christ in the Supper from the Christ we get in the Word. But we may well get the same Christ better as the Spirit ministers by the testimony of the physical emblems being joined to the Word.

Basing their thinking on an allegorical understanding of the Song of Solomon, Christian writers in the past have spoken of the 'kiss' of Christ. This is the secret ministry of the Spirit. Just as the action of a kiss communicates and symbolises love, so the physical emblems which point to a crucified and risen Saviour are employed by the Spirit working in the heart to communicate to Christ's people the love he has for them. The Supper is used in the hands of the Spirit to minister peace, joy, love and assurance. There can be a foretaste of the fullness of the presence of Christ which the believer anticipates as he proclaims Christ's death until he comes. When Christ comes, the regenerating work of the Spirit will be fully consummated and the full reality expressed by the symbols will be present.

Here then is a brief snapshot of Calvin's doctrine of the Holy Spirit. It is the Spirit who unites us to Christ by faith and who grants us assurance of salvation. It is the Spirit who authenticates the Bible as the Word of God and who in the sacrament of the Lord's Supper makes Christ's presence real to us. This doctrine of the Spirit is full and rounded and nuanced. No one can ever say that with regard to John Calvin the Holy Spirit is the forgotten or unknown member of the Trinity.

CHAPTER 7

'*Ardens sed Virens* – Burning but Flourishing': Open to the Spirit of Christ who rejuvenates the Church

Liam M. Tracey

'*Ardens sed Virens* - burning but flourishing' was the general title for this session of our conference. The title is taken from the motto of the Irish Presbyterian Church which usually includes the symbol of the burning bush of Exodus 3.[1] Dr Stafford Carson has spoken on the role of the Holy Spirit in sustaining the Church's life.

While no one here presents doubts that the scattered Church of Christ is in constant need of renewal and rejuvenation, is there something in the back of the organisers' collective mind that links this with the celebration of the liturgy of the Church? Of course, to ask such a question of a liturgist is already to have answered it: it is in the celebration of the liturgy and in our praise and invocation of the living God that the Church is rejuvenated. It often happens that when people learn that I am a liturgist, that I have spent a good part of my life studying liturgy and now spend a great deal of my life teaching the subject, they immediately seek answers, or express opinions or want a

---

1. For a historical sketch of its origins and use, see the article by the Rev. Robert Cobain on the website of the Irish Presbyterian Church http://www.presbyterianireland.org/about/bush1.html (accessed 30 June 2011).

127

particular insight (or what might appear to me to be a prejudice) endorsed, agreed with or even praised.

Confusion over where to slot me is another common experience: 'Are you a historian,' they wonder, 'or a theologian or a social scientist?' Then they usually move onto the joke about the difference between a liturgist and a terrorist, which I usually counter with a less well-known one about the difference between the liturgist and the systematic theologian ('a liturgist doesn't care how many persons are in the blessed Trinity as long as everyone is standing in the right place').

The invitation to participate in this conference provoked in me something that is a frequent inner debate. It runs something like: What is liturgical study actually engaged in? What are the presuppositions that I come with as a liturgist? In speaking with you today, I also ask about the presuppositions those who invite a liturgist to a conference or a consultation or indeed a parish group bring with their invitation. To put it more bluntly, why might I be considered an apt person to address the topic at hand, and even more centrally, what are you expecting me to say and ultimately what would you like me to confirm for you?

If it is indeed Christ who is the one who rejuvenates and makes new the Church, it is the liturgical celebration where this work of newness takes place. Liturgy as the celebration of the recapitulation of events of salvation in the person of Jesus Christ means that, for the disciple, every moment, every place and every event have found in him their fulfilment. In Christ the events of creation and its endpoint find their centrifugal point. True worship, the worship desire by God in spirit and in truth, is the living, dying and rising of Jesus Christ. This is the worship that every Christian community is called to offer as it celebrates its newness in Christ. As Paul reminded the Roman community:

'I implore you by God's mercy to offer your very selves to him: a living sacrifice consecrated and fit for his acceptance; *this is your authentic worship*' (Romans 12:1). It is clear from Paul's writings that for him, liturgy (the life of worship) and the living of the Christian message are one and the same. Liturgy, sacrifice, priest, offering are words all used in connection with a life of self giving that takes Jesus as its model. The worship of the Church is to build up the body of Christ as it becomes ever more what it is called to be – the community of faith immersed in the Risen Lord. Liturgy, as we are reminded by Leo the Great, is the presence of the Lord among us, as it is nothing more than 'what was visible in our Redeemer now passed into the mysteries (celebrations) of the Church'.[2] The Church is called to carry on the ministry of Jesus in the celebration of the liturgy. Liturgy then is not an act of private devotion or piety: it is first and foremost an activity of God in Christ Jesus. The saving work of Christ continues throughout the centuries in the activity of the Church of which he is the head. So liturgy is the common work of Christ and his Church. This foundational principle grounds the audacious claims that the Roman Catholic Church make about the nature of Christian worship. Near the beginning of *Sacrosanctum Concilium*, Vatican II's Constitution on the Liturgy, we read: 'it is the liturgy through which ... the work of our redemption is accomplished'.[3] This was of course building on the 1947 encyclical letter of Pius XII, *Mediator Dei*, an early highpoint of the modern liturgical movement. Not only did this letter affirm that the work of redemption is accomplished

---

2. St Leo the Great, 'On the Lord's Ascension', Sermon 74, 2.

3. 'The Constitution on the Sacred Liturgy' in *The Basic Sixteen Documents of Vatican Council II*, ed. Austin Flannery O.P. (Dublin: Dominican Publications, 1996), 117–61.

through the celebration of the liturgy, it also noted that the public prayer of the Church is superior to private prayer. These key insights of Pius XII not only confirmed the work of the liturgical movement against many Roman (and indeed Jesuit) detractors: they also laid the groundwork for the first great document of the Second Vatican Council, the 'Constitution on the Sacred Liturgy', issued in 1963 with its insistence that the liturgy is the source and summit of the activity of the Church.

This viewpoint on the liturgy is of course a contemporary one that has been informed by over a century of work and reflection by the modern liturgical movement and has influenced all of our Christian communities.[4] It is of course not how liturgy was understood at the time of our two honourees, Ignatius of Loyola and John Calvin. As Robert Taft has remarked, the liturgical life of the Church in which Ignatius lived was in the 'throes of the most degenerate period of its liturgical history'.[5] The liturgical life of the community as it had been experienced in Late Antiquity and even the early Middle Ages was now at an end. The bishop's role as the chief liturgical minister on behalf of a community was no longer evident; priests were no longer ordained for a particular ecclesial community and many seemed more interested in their own spiritual entertainment and gathering mass stipends. The sense that the cathedral, with its baptistery, was central to the liturgical life of the diocese had been forgotten. We see an ever greater fragmentation of liturgical unity and an increasing privatisation of the celebration

---

4. Many see the work of the modern liturgical movement as a retrieval of patristic concepts and ideas.

5. Robert F. Taft, SJ, 'Liturgy in the Life and Mission of the Society of Jesus', in Keith Pecklers, SJ, *Liturgy in a Postmodern World* (London: Continuum, 2003), 38.

of the Eucharist. The eucharistic prayer proclaimed in silence opened the door for evermore fantastical and allegorical explanations of the Mass. The Eucharist was something to be seen, and certainly not something to be received in the form of communion. Adoration displaced in many ways the Mass itself and laid the ground for later Baroque developments. The Liturgy of the Hours had grown beyond all control and its celebration in many places seems to have been less than edifying. The Council of Trent reacted to these trends but, as Klauser has noted, it was at the cost of 'rigid unification'.[6] Liturgy for the Council of Trent, and in the centuries following, was an affair of externals, in that it was largely taken up with rubrics or ceremonial. It was discussed in terms of validity, something that 'worked' and, for those who placed no obstacle in its way, it 'produced grace'. What counted was the matter and form of the sacrament celebrated. The celebrative nature was nice but not essential, useful in that it might stir the faithful to confession but nothing more. For spiritual nourishment, the faithful turned elsewhere – to private piety, devotions, missions, retreats, etc. The long march that saw the Christian life as something private continued and in many cases quickened its pace. As a result of this process, the sense of our communal nature as Church, as the Body of Christ, that we are saved as a social body, was weakened and even obscured. Liturgy was seen fundamentally as the communication of grace to an individual soul and its relationship with a life of faith and membership of the Church was not reflected upon.

------

6. Theodor Klauser, *A Short History of the Western Liturgy. An Account and some Reflections*, 2nd ed. (Oxford: Oxford University Press, 1979), 117. The fourth chapter of Klauser deals with the reaction of the Council of Trent to the challenges of the reformers, interestingly Calvin is not mentioned by Klauser.

The devotional life of Christians continued to be focused on the person of Jesus through a proliferation of devotions and meditative practices. This led increasingly away from the traditional public offices of the Church and towards a flowering of interior private prayer already evident in the Rhenish and Flemish mystics of the previous centuries. When Ignatius dispensed with or kept to a minimum what may have seemed to him to be the formalistic and ritualistic dimensions of religious life, it was as a result of this long privatisation of prayer.[7] For him liturgy and sacraments were instruments of personal holiness: even the celebration of the Eucharist was a personal and private thing. Ignatius had no proper appreciation of the liturgy and there is no use trying to prove that he did.[8] But as has already emerged in our conversation, the fundamental elements of his, and of Calvin's vision as well, is the goal at which we wish to arrive. It is the spirit of the Risen Christ who will rejuvenate the Church. This awareness that Jesus is Lord, not of the past, but of contemporary history, is the aim of all Christian spirituality and liturgical anamnesis. The life, death and resurrection of Jesus are past events in that they happened in the past, but they are eternally present in God and are present to us in Christ Jesus. Others have remarked upon the extraordinary contemporary feel to many aspects of Ignatius's teaching, for example, the centrality of the Trinity and his focus on the Risen Christ

7. While Ignatius and the early Jesuits are perhaps the most famous examples of this new form of prayer in religious life, they were not the first. It was a movement that even affected monastic reform movements, as Salvador Ryan has shown in the second chapter of this collection.

8. See R. Taft's 'Liturgy in the Life and Mission of the Society of Jesus' (footnote 5 above) as an invaluable introduction to Ignatius's understanding of the liturgy of the Church.

present in the life of the Church. But Christian life and mission cannot be reduced solely to liturgy and its celebration, so the late monastic influences which weighed heavy in even more recently founded religious orders had to be removed if a new kind of religious life was to flourish. Ignatius was part of a wider reaction against such an external view of liturgy. It is a reaction that shares much with the Protestant reformers, or perhaps it might be more accurate to say that what was being rejected by both was an overblown medieval ritualism.[9]

Ignatius was following a well-worn path, trodden by many others, in reducing the quantity of liturgy required for the members of his Society. Robert Taft, in an exhaustive study of early Jesuits and liturgy, concludes that if we want to know what liturgy was for Ignatius, we should concentrate on ministry and mission, something that characterises both the Catholic and Protestant Reforms.[10] It is the ministry of God's Word that dominates both Protestant and early Jesuit sources. This was then taken up by the Council of Trent which sees the ministry of the Word and its preaching as the chief task of bishops. What was not clear to Ignatius because of the time and place in which he lived, was that liturgy is public and communitarian by its nature: salvation is not an individual event but one that happens in the Body of Christ that we call the Church.

---

9. Taft, 'Liturgy in the Life', 43: Ignatius grasped intuitively, however, that not everything in Christian life can be reduced to liturgy, and liturgy under the weight of monastic influence has tended in both East and West to swallow up everything else. Ignatian views on prayer are part of reaction against medieval externalism and ritualistic sacramentalism that the sixteenth-century Catholic reform movement shared with Protestant reformers.

10. Robert Taft, 'Jesuit Liturgy – An Oxymoron?' *Worship* 84 (2010), 38–70.

BEGINNING WITH THE HUMAN

The object of liturgical studies is the meaning of the liturgical celebration, to begin with the question: why do we humans celebrate, or what is it in the human person that leads individuals and communities to celebrate? It is only after reflecting on this fundamental question that we can move on to examine how we do in fact celebrate. The passage from 'why' to 'how' is crucial to the reading of liturgical history and theology. For then the 'why' of the liturgical experience constantly informs and challenges 'how' concrete Christian communities celebrate the liturgy. This is not to negate in any way the theological nature of the liturgical action or to reduce Christian liturgy merely to another kind of ritual possibility. It is, rather, to take seriously that liturgy is a ritual mediation of the mystery of Christ and to use any method that will aid the study of the celebratory nature of the liturgy.

Contemporary liturgical reform and renewal has sometimes suffered from accusations that it begins with the worshipping subject, or the gathering of the people of God; that it pays too much attention to those who gather and, even worse, that the liturgy has become a means of therapy, or the confirmation of their worldview by the members of a cosy clique. This viewpoint can be found not only among those who oppose liturgical reform, but it may also be found in the work of those who are deeply committed to liturgical renewal but who are convinced that much of what has passed for liturgical renewal is merely middle-class chatter. Liturgical renewal as conceived mainly in North America, but with knock-on effects in this part of the world, has sometimes fostered closed communities and done little to open them to the challenge of the gospel *ordo* (or structure) supposedly present in the liturgical celebration.[11] Liturgical reformers are sometimes accused of having adapted the liturgy to the prevailing culture but of doing little or nothing to maintain its extrinsic strangeness. Obviously if liturgy is approached from the view of the subject (the individual worshipper or the worshipping community), a greater openness to change and reform is present. Liturgy can be seen as something that is deeply cultural, reflecting the worldviews and thoughts of the milieu out of which it has emerged, and therefore allowing for change now and into the future. In short, it is open to the possibility of reform and inculturation. A classic and helpful example of this approach is the parable told by an Indian Jesuit entitled 'Ashram Cats':

> When the guru sat down to worship each evening, the ashram cat would get in the way and distract the worshipers. So he ordered that the cat be tied during evening worship. After the guru died, the cat continued to be tied during evening worship. And when the cat died, another cat was brought to the ashram so that it could be duly tied during evening worship. Centuries later learned treatises were written by the guru's disciples on the religious and liturgical significance of tying up a cat while worship is performed.[12]

---

11. The work of the late lamented Mark Searle is particularly helpful in this regard, see Mark Searle, *Called to Participate. Theological, Ritual and Social Perspectives* (Collegeville: The Liturgical Press, 2006).

12. Anthony de Mello, 'The Guru's Cat', in *The Song of the Bird* (Doubleday: New York, 1982), 63.

OR STARTING WITH THE DIVINE?

In reaction to what is seen by some as a too heavily subject-focused liturgical renewal, some have called for a return to a greater God-focus in liturgical renewal. This is a perspective where liturgy is very much conceived as a given, as something to be embraced and which judges the world, not the other way around. A recent address by the Archbishop of Denver, Charles Chaput, illustrates this viewpoint well:

> The project is not shaping the liturgy according to the suppositions of the age, but allowing the liturgy to question and shape the suppositions of any age. Is the modern man incapable of the liturgical act? Probably. But this is no ground for despair. Our goal is not to accommodate the liturgy to the world, but to let the liturgy be itself – a transformative icon of the *ordo* of God.

> Barron suggests that in the post-conciliar era, the professional Catholic liturgical establishment opted for the former path, trying to adapt the liturgy to the demands of modern culture. I would agree. And I would add that time has shown this to be a dead end. Trying to engineer the liturgy to be more 'relevant' and 'intelligible' through a kind of relentless cult of novelty, has only resulted in confusion and a deepening of the divide between believers and the true spirit of the liturgy.[13]

---

13. Charles Chaput, *Glorify God by Your life: Evangelization and the Renewal of the Liturgy.* Hillenbrand Lecture, 24 June 2010 at the Liturgical Institute, Mundelin, Chicago. See www.archden.org/index. cfm/ID/4113.

For those who share this viewpoint, the call is to return to a sense of mystery and transcendence that is often linked to a solemn liturgy celebrated in a highly formalised language and style and, for some, preferably in Latin. They would reject any attempt at inculturating the liturgy and would regard any accommodation with contemporary culture as a betrayal of the liturgy which they construct over against contemporary culture. Not all of those who favour such a view of liturgy would support a return to the so-called 'Extraordinary Form' of the celebration of the Eucharist in the Roman Catholic Church. Many do, and they claim that their greatest support is among young people who are leading the way in the desire for the 'Extraordinary Form'. Those who do support the Ordinary Form are often seen as middle-aged *Tablet* readers who have not moved on with the times and embraced the new cyber age in which we live with postmodernity and medieval liturgy existing together.

LITURGY WARS

Roman Catholic liturgical reform, which began with the Second Vatican Council, is now over forty years old: someone remarked recently that we have another seventy years to go. Much of the work of the reform has taken place, what concerns many now is whether it has led to a renewal of worship. Some would claim it has, while others would be inclined to give a very definite negative answer to this question. Increasingly we hear talk of a 'reform of the reform' or alternative views of the modern liturgical movement and its struggles during the last century. This has led to what some have called 'liturgy wars'. Crucial questions to both sides in this so-called war, are 'What was the reform about?' and 'Has what has actually taken place honoured and responded to liturgical reform and renewal, or has it wandered far from the intentions of those early liturgical reformers and the calls of Vatican II?' What is at issue in many of these discussions is precisely the topic of renewal and reform as expressed, for example, in questions such as 'Who might be responsible for the work of reform?', 'Can it be rolled back?' and 'What must be held onto?'

In January 2010, Benedictine Fr Anscar J. Chupungco, director of the Paul VI Institute of Liturgy in the Philippines and former president of the Pontifical Liturgical Institute at Sant'Anselmo in Rome, gave a stinging critique of the 'reform of the reform', a phrase used weeks earlier by none other than the papal master of ceremonies, Msgr Guido Marini. In a talk at the launch of a program in liturgical studies at Australia's University of Newcastle, Chupungco responded to Marini's claim that the Vatican II liturgical reform has 'not always in its practical implementation found a timely and happy fulfilment'.[14] 'What are the possible implications of a reform of the postconciliar reform?' Chupungco asked. 'What remedy does it offer for a reform that according to some Catholics has gone bad? What agenda does it put forward so that liturgical worship could be more reverent and prayerful?' The liturgy envisioned by the council, he stated,

> was marked by noble simplicity and clarity. It wanted a liturgy that the people could easily follow. In sharp contrast is the

14. Anscar J. Chupungco, OSB, *Liturgical Studies and Liturgical Renewal,* a paper read on the occasion of the launch of The Broken Bay Institute – University of Newcastle's Graduate Certificate in Theology, 21 January 2010, Sydney, Australia. The lecture can be found at www. praytellblog. com/index.php/tag/chupungco. He returns to many of these themes in a fuller study, see Anscar J. Chupungco, *What, Then, Is Liturgy? Musings and Memoir* (Collegeville: The Liturgical Press, 2010).

attempt to revive, at the expense of active participation, the medieval usage that was espoused by the Tridentine [or pre-Vatican II] rite and to retrieve eagerly the liturgical paraphernalia that had been deposited in museums as historical artefacts.

Comparing the reforms of Vatican II to a springtime renewal, Chupungco lamented that, more than four decades on, 'the Church is now experiencing the cold chill of winter brought about by contrasting ideas of what the liturgy is and how it should be celebrated'. Such tension, he said, 'could be a healthy sign that the interest in the liturgy has not abated'. He cautioned, however, that after the council, 'we are not free to propound views' apart from principles established by the council:

> ... there are surely instances of postconciliar implementation that are debatable, but we should be careful to distinguish them from the conciliar principles, especially the full, active participation of all God's people in the liturgy.

LITURGY AND THE WORK OF RENEWAL

A central contention of this paper is that the liturgy and its celebration are essential to the renewal of the Christian community. Liturgy is seen as the ongoing active presence of the Risen Christ in the midst of the community: gathering and sanctifying the people of God, proclaiming and blessing the wonders of God even now, giving thanks and sending forth from the tables of the Word and the Sacrament. This saving presence in Word, Sacrament, Minister and People is the ongoing work of the Holy Spirit.

These central theological insights and concerns can be lost sight of in the task of altering and adapting our modes of worship or of renewing and reforming our liturgy. Each Christian community is called to improve constantly the quality of its liturgical celebration, to create the best place for this celebration and to open and sustain a sense of welcome and hospitality to their brothers and sisters. Some Christian traditions have put much effort into experimenting with new styles of liturgy that draw on popular music and instrumentation. Rather than looking for innovation, however, the way to better worship lies in a renewed commitment to doing the basics well: training readers so that the Scriptures are proclaimed with clarity and conviction; forming people with musical talent so that the parish's liturgical music inspires faith; creating a worship space which enables the full, conscious and active participation of all present; purchasing good quality liturgical vestments and vessels which show that what we celebrate is of great value and significance to us; giving high priority to the time the preacher needs to prepare a weekly homily that engages people and relates to the realities of current life.

In the Roman Catholic tradition, since the liturgical reforms of Vatican II, we have been inclined to use the Eucharist as a 'one stop' ritual, suitable for 'all sorts and conditions' of the worshipping community. It may be the only liturgical experience that a local parish offers to its parishioners. While not disputing the fact that the celebration of the Eucharist is indeed the highpoint of the liturgical life of the Church, it is not, nor was it intended to be, the only form of worship. The celebration of the Eucharist requires a certain liturgical fluency and even literacy. It expects that those participating are familiar with its structure and flow, its use of language and symbol. For those joining our communities for the first time or for those who only have occasional contact with them, the Eucharist may not be the place to welcome them or be the style of worship that will immediately appeal to them. Christian communities need to reflect on the kinds of worship they offer and indeed the opportunities they provide for the celebration of the daily divine office, celebrations of the Word and other liturgical gatherings. These moments of prayer can enable people to feel more at home with the formal grammar of Christian prayer and provide an entry point into participating in the liturgy and ritual of the community. The Sunday homily and other moments for preaching can be a useful way of informing, encouraging and teaching the assembly how to pray publicly as a community. Parish websites, newsletters and other means of communication, can offer ways of enabling all of the assembly to become more familiar with words and gestures of worship.

Liturgy is the source and summit of all we are and do as Christians. We need its ongoing support to sustain and strengthen our mission in the world; we all need to be nourished regularly at the table of the Word and the table of the Eucharist. Faith weakens over time without the support of a worshipping and living community where the Spirit of the Risen Christ is working and acting.

Worshipping with a community of fellow believers takes us beyond ourselves so that we become part of something bigger, part of the Church, the Body of Christ, members of his ongoing praise of the Father, participating truly in his priestly work that is celebrated by others in every corner of the world and which has been celebrated by men and women of faith for over two thousand years. This is nothing short of being caught up in the action of the Risen Christ who constantly rejuvenates and renews his Church.

141

CHAPTER 8

Calvin and Mission

Drew Gibson

'In the Protestant world, during the period of the Reformation there was little time for thought of missions.'[1] One hates to disagree with a bishop, especially a bishop who wrote the definitive short history of mission, but I have to question Stephen Neill's assertion. You see, it all depends on what you mean by 'mission'. If you take Neill's understanding of mission as something like 'evangelisation and planting of the Church among those peoples and groups where she has not yet taken root', as defined in the Second Vatican Council's Decree on Missions (*Ad Gentes,* 1965), then he is right. But, if we adopt a much fuller understanding of mission, then he is clearly wrong. In my opinion, John Stott's definition has yet to be bettered: 'everything that the Church is sent into the world to do.'[2] The Reformers believed that they were doing the work of God, commissioned by him, in the world, so it can be argued that the work of Reformation itself was conceived missionally. But, we are now in danger of casting the net too wide. Let us settle on a more technical definition of mission: 'that activity of the Church that takes place at its interface with the world, that is, with all that is not God Himself or the Church itself'.

---

1. Stephen Neill, *A History of Christian Missions* (Harmondsworth: Penguin, 1964), 220.

2. John Stott, *Christian Mission in the Modern World* (London: Falcon, 1975), 30.

In agreement with the other Reformers, John Calvin believed that there was a huge problem with the Church. It was not just that there was immorality among the clergy or lethargy in high places or even inaccurate teaching. The problem that he saw was that the Church had lost its missionary role and hence, as Vatican II much later pointed out, had denied its very nature. In his opinion, the Church was no longer living and proclaiming the true Gospel, therefore it was not aligned with the mission of God, and so it could no longer claim to truly be a Church. Although he would not have used the term, he would have said that his work of Reformation was the attempt to produce a truly 'missional' Church.

But Calvin's total work was missional in another way also. If the Church was not proclaiming the Gospel, then much of Europe was 'unreached'. People had not had the opportunity to hear the Gospel and therefore Reformation was a necessary first step to authentic evangelisation. Although his work was done within Christendom and he could quite happily use the term 'Christian' in a broad cultural sense, he still perceived large numbers of individuals and whole communities as 'unreached'. He sought to establish a Church in Geneva that was truly missional and, as we shall see, arguably all of his work is best understood through that lens. Before we look at Calvin's missionary practice, let us look first at Calvin's theology.

CALVIN'S THEOLOGY OF MISSION

Calvin's theology is best understood as a missionary theology. It is ordered around two poles: a strong sense of the glory of God and a great compassion for the salvation of human beings. These two themes dominate all his writings, either clearly on their surface or as part of their substructure, and these two are at the heart of any serious missionary theology. But these two 'roots' bear a wide variety of fruit and perhaps the most important work on mission of the past generation, by David Bosch, has clearly shown that mission is never to be understood narrowly, within a social utopianism, an individualistic pietism, a cultural ghettoism or an ecclesiastical imperialism.[3] As we expand our understanding of mission, so we will appreciate the degree to which it is appropriate to honour John Calvin's contribution to it. Let us engage with some of the most prominent twentieth-century theologians to demonstrate this.

i. Calvin and Missio Dei

Between the First and Second World Wars, Karl Barth and Karl Hartenstein introduced a fuller understanding of *Missio Dei*, the mission of God, than had been accepted for many generations. They reminded us that mission is of the essence of the nature of God.[4] God is a missionary being and only when we understand this can we fully understand the nature of Christian mission. God is sovereignly and freely at work in his world in ways that go far beyond and are completely unrelated to the institutional Church. The notion of *Missio Dei* is the foundation of the Vatican II documents that focus on mission, most notably the decree, *Ad Gentes*.[5] The key pillars of Calvin's theology are also key pillars of these documents in so far as they reflect the *Missio Dei*. Notice the similarities in some foundational theological commitments. It is fascinating to note how themes that are at

---

3. David Bosch, *Transforming Mission* (Maryknoll: Orbis, 1991).

4. Stephen Bevans and Roger Schroeder, *Constants in Context* (Maryknoll: Orbis, 2004), 290.

5. Decree on the Church's Missionary Activity (*Ad Gentes*), ET in A. Flannery, ed., *Vatican Council II: The Conciliar and Post Conciliar Documents* (Dublin: Dominican Publication, 1975), 813–62.

the heart of Calvin's theology are used to support the missional thrust of *Ad Gentes* and, in one example, *Gaudium et Spes*.

ii. God is sovereign over all the earth

Calvin speaks of God 'who, of his own wisdom, from the remotest eternity, decreed what he would do, and now by his own power executes what he has decreed.'[6] *Ad Gentes* draws out a missiological conclusion from this premise: 'Missionary activity is nothing else and nothing less than an epiphany, or a manifesting of God's decree, and its fulfilment in the world and in world history' (*Ad Gentes*, 9).

iii. God reveals himself in the world outside the Church

Both Calvin and the Council recognised the humbling truth that the Church does not define the limits of God's activity in the world, so that Calvin maintains that 'we cannot open our eyes without being compelled to behold him' (*Institutes,* I.v.1). Indeed, for Calvin, the very revelation of God in creation, and especially in the human conscience, is why human beings cannot claim innocence and need to be the objects of mission. *Gaudium et Spes* speaks of 'the Lord's Spirit, who fills the earth' (11). God is not confined to the institution of the Church and, indeed, if He was not universally present, there would be no inclination towards or hunger for the Gospel, carried by the missionaries of the Church.

iv. The glory of God is the end of all creation

Calvin says that the ultimate end of all things is not to be found in things themselves but in their relationship to God himself. Of the Church he says: 'the whole object contemplated in

---

6. John Calvin, *Institutes of the Christian Religion* (Florida: MacDonald, 1971), I.xvi.8. References in text are to this edition.

our election is, that 'we should be to the praise of his glory' (*Institutes,* III.xxii.3).

Again *Ad Gentes* puts this same idea into a missionary context when it says: 'it is God who brings it about ... that ... the nations may soon be led to the knowledge of the truth (1 Tim 2:4) and the glory of God ...'(*Ad Gentes*, 42).

v. The Gospel is to be proclaimed worldwide

This last connection of Calvin with *Missio Dei*, through the documents of Vatican 11, is one that warms the hearts of all Evangelical Christians. Calvin's theology most clearly shows in the man, a burning desire to have the Gospel proclaimed throughout the earth. In other words, he was committed to evangelism. He says: 'for it is our duty to proclaim the goodness of God to every nation ... the work is such as ought not to be concealed in a corner, but to be everywhere proclaimed'.[7] With no less passion, the Council says:

> The mission of the Church, therefore, is fulfilled by that activity which makes her ... fully present to all men or nations, in order that ... she may lead them to the faith, the freedom and the peace of Christ ... (*Ad Gentes*, 5).

vi. Calvin's interaction with contemporary culture

Calvin's theology is also missionary in another way and to understand this aspect we turn to a second bishop, Lesslie Newbigin. Newbigin's missionary life was largely spent in India. On his retirement to his native England he found a society that, in

---

7. Comment on Is. 12:5, cited in Scott Simmons, *John Calvin and Missions: A Historical Study* (2003) http://www.aplacefortruth.org/calvin.missions1.htm (accessed 20 October, 2010).

his opinion, had almost entirely lost its connection with its historic Christian roots. His later years were dominated by his desire to communicate the Gospel to this society and to contemporary western culture in general. Newbigin reminded us that the whole point of doing theology is to communicate the Gospel to contemporary culture, in other words, to express eternal truth in ways that contemporary culture could understand. In *The Other Side of 1984: Questions to the Churches*, Newbigin called the Church to explore the relationship between the Gospel and the fiduciary framework in which that Gospel is proclaimed and lived.[8]

In Calvin's time, the Renaissance, the rise of humanism, the development of the independent city state and many other social forces had brought about an increasing gulf between sixteenth-century thinking on life as a whole and sixteenth-century thinking about Christian faith, which was still formally rooted in the Medieval era. David Meredith puts it like this:

How was the Reformation exciting? It got the Church back to work; the Medieval Church was simply not capable of relating to the needs and concerns of the modern world. The new Church engages and enthuses the laity and sees the potential of the cities. These were men and women who drank new wine and who witnessed the old wineskins bursting with glorious new life. The Reformation also produced an army of great thinkers quite simply because it revealed a great God. Calvin sought to bridge this gap.[9]

---

8. Lesslie Newbigin, *The Other Side of 1984: Questions to the Churches* (Geneva: World Council of Churches, 1983).

9. David Meredith, unpublished paper (Edinburgh, 2010).

As a trained lawyer and classical scholar, Calvin used the best contemporary intellectual tools in his commitment to understanding Scripture and in communicating this understanding to his contemporaries.

Calvin's theology breathed the same air as the rest of his intellectual contemporaries. His whole approach to the study of written texts reflected the intellectual humanism within which Erasmus, for example, worked. He spoke harshly of philosophy, not as one who knew little but as one who wanted to keep that which he knew in its proper place. Because he passionately wanted all people to hear God speaking with clarity, he did not allow any philosophical system, either contemporary or from antiquity, to be the matrix within which he did his theology. On the other hand he was happy to draw from the philosophers anything that he could use to help him express his theology with clarity. In other words, he used, but was not bound by, contemporary intellectual culture. Or, to put it in more missiological terms, he engaged missionally with contemporary intellectual culture, understanding it in order to appropriate what is good in it for his higher purpose and rejecting all in it that inhibited the communication of the Gospel. Calvin's view of culture is well summarised as 'wishing, quite explicitly, to consider the various arts as maid-servants. He cautions against making them mistresses.'[10]

vii. Calvin and Liberation

A final insight into the missionary nature of Calvin's theology comes via the Latin American theologian, Gustavo Gutierrez.

---

10. For an interesting and curiously sympathetic perspective on Calvin and Philosophy see Holder's essay http://www.iep.utm.edu/calvin/ (accessed 2 October, 2010).

Gutierrez critiqued Eurocentric, academic theologies that only served to alienate the church from the real lives of real people.[11] He maintained that true theology illuminates the minds of ordinary people to identify all that oppresses and destroys them. A conversation between Calvin and Gutierrez would have been fascinating. Despite their profound differences, both would agree that theology expresses ultimate truth in ways that form minds and ultimately set people free. To be sure, the professional theologian has his or her place but reflective theology is only part of a larger project which is the liberation of persons and communities from the ravages of sin both eternally and in the here and now.

Thus, Calvin was concerned with the whole life of Geneva. His understanding of a fully reformed faith was that it 'applies equally to our minds as to our hands' (*Institutes,* II.viii.45) and therefore he engaged in ordering the governance of Geneva, relief for refugees and the poor and the improvement of living conditions in the city. Lee informs us that, following Calvin's establishment as a dominant force in Geneva, 'Short-changing merchants were punished. Begging was prohibited. Jobs were created, to help the unemployed. Sewers were installed, to combat disease. Dentists were tested and licensed to pull teeth.'[12] He debated often and on many subjects. His correspondence was voluminous and his interest in the total life of the city of Geneva brought him into more conflict with the city council than did many of his theological proposals.

---

11. Gustavo Gutierrez, *A Theology of Liberation* (London: SCM, 1974).

12. F.N. Lee, *The Godly Life of John Calvin* (16 November, 1985). http://www.dr-fnlee.org/docs4/tglojc/tglojc.pdf (accessed 2 October, 2010).

All contemporary missiologists agree that mission is hamstrung if the missional community from which it springs is not committed to arresting social decay, addressing the needs of the poor and dispossessed, and engaging with all of the incursions of sin into the life of the whole community. Calvin had this commitment.

CALVIN'S MISSIONARY ACTIVITY
i. Printing

While not a missionary endeavour in itself, the invention of the printing press had huge consequences for the mission of the Church, and in Calvin's Geneva the value of the printed word was not underestimated. At the time of his death, the city had thirty-four printing presses with an annual capacity of over a quarter of a million books.[13] Virtually every missionary society and board of the modern era has recognised the value of the printed word for mission but, obviously one specific aspect of printing is foremost: the production of Bibles, especially in the vernacular. Calvin was not unaware of this.

ii. Translation of Scripture

While Luther's German translation of the Bible is better known, Calvin's support for the translation of the Bible into vernacular languages produced two very significant works: the Geneva Bible (1557, the work of William Whittingham, Calvin's brother in law) and Olivétan's Bible (the first French translation was published in 1535 – Olivétan was possibly Calvin's cousin). Calvin wrote a preface for Olivetan's first edition but he was also

---

13. Michael A. J. Haykin. *'A Sacrifice Well Pleasing To God': John Calvin and the Missionary Endeavour of the Church* (2009). https://www.galaxie.com/article/16719 (accessed 20 October, 2010).

involved in revisions that took place subsequently in Geneva. Obviously translation of the Bible into the vernacular has been a hugely missionary enterprise for as long as the Bible has existed.

iii. Church planting in France and elsewhere in Europe

There were several distinct aspects to Calvin's work of church planting and expansion in Europe. We shall consider them briefly under two heads:

a. Ministering to refugees

Perhaps the most obvious and important missionary endeavour of John Calvin was his enthusiastic support for planting churches in his native France. Calvin had first come to Geneva as a refugee from France, so it is no surprise that he had a special concern for refugees from his home country and elsewhere and that he saw huge opportunities in equipping those refugees to return home with the Gospel. Exact numbers are hard to discern but certainly Geneva hosted many thousands of refugees, not only from France but from virtually the whole of Catholic Europe. One figure is 'slightly more than 21,000'.[14] Among the most famous of the refugees was John Knox, whose greatest achievements were in Scotland. Significant work was also done by refugees returning to England, Holland, Poland and Hungary. Today, much Christian work continues among refugees, not only humanitarian relief work but evangelism, Christian training, even fairly high-level theological education.

b. Training Church planters

While refugees were given shelter and fellowship, in 1559 a

---

14. Ibid.

college was founded, one of the objects of which was to train ministers to go back to their home countries as 'reformers' or church planters. Again numbers are difficult to assess but the following are generally accepted. In 1555, there were five Reformed Churches in France; in 1559 there were fewer than one hundred, but in 1562 there were approximately 2,150. In 1561 alone, 142 ministers were sent from Geneva to France. By any standards this is remarkable growth and the claim that, at the time of Calvin's death, one tenth of the population were members of Reformed Churches is the most conservative that I have come across.

Today, theologians such as Tim Keller, Mark Driscoll and C. Peter Wagner claim that, following the demise of Christendom, the presence of many church buildings and worshipping congregations gives a false impression of the extent of the presence of the Church. Calvin would have said that the same was true of his day. The presence of church buildings and people meeting for Christian activities is not a guarantee of the presence of a vital Church and offers no reason why a truly vibrant new Church should not be planted.

iv. Church planting in Brazil

In 1555 Nicholas Durand, a French nobleman, who had studied with Calvin in Paris, led a colonial expedition to Brazil. He had sympathies for the Reform movement and sent a request back to France for some spiritual support. The request found its way to Geneva and in the following year two pastors and eleven laymen were commissioned and set sail, arriving in what is now Rio de Janeiro in March 1557. However, all did not go well. Within a year relationships had soured, Durand became hostile, three of the Genevans died (possibly murdered) and the rest returned to Europe. The enterprise was a failure yet, even here, there were hints of a pattern of mission that had been familiar to Catholics for generations and that would soon be established among Protestants. When missionaries travelled with traders, soldiers and colonial officials there was always the potential for fruitful cooperation but, sadly, history has proved that the links too often were actually toxic to the Gospel.

v. Mission through the leaders of society taking up their responsibilities

Among the many hundreds of letters written by Calvin throughout his life is a significant number to monarchs, princes and persons of nobility. These include the dedicatory epistles in his major works. For example, his commentary on John's Gospel is dedicated as follows: 'To the right honourable lords the syndics and senate of Geneva and his respected lords, John Calvin prays from the Lord the Spirit of wisdom and strength and success in government.'[15] Calvin did not always enjoy harmonious relationships with the Geneva city council, especially in his early years in the city, but he was sure that their work was 'spiritual'. They had responsibilities given to them by God and the work of the Council was an appropriate means by which Christian people could express their faith. As such, it is missional. As André Bieler says, 'The state exercised control over the institution's material goods, but the men allotted to this work conducted a real ecclesiastical ministry.'[16]

---

15. John Calvin (trans. by THL Parker), *The Gospel According to St John 1-10* (Edinburgh: St Andrew Press, 1959), 1.

16. André Bieler, *Calvin's Economic and Social Thought* (Geneva: WARC, 2005), 135.

Contemporary missiology includes in its brief the extension of the reign of God into all areas of life. This includes addressing structural and political evils of all kinds. When seen in this context, Calvin's concern about building a just and humane society in Geneva can be fairly understood as missional and his support for many other secular rulers in their endeavours to lead their people is rightly interpreted as promoting the *Mission Dei*.

vi. Evangelistic preaching

Calvin was committed to evangelistic preaching both in theory and in practice. He wrote:

> ... although he is able to accomplish the secret work of his Holy Spirit without any means or assistance, he has nevertheless ordained outward preaching, to use it as it were as a means. But to make such a means effective and fruitful he inscribes in our hearts with his own finger those very words which he speaks in our ears by the mouth of a human being.[17]

It is impossible to read Calvin's sermons without being struck by his passion that men and women should submit themselves to Jesus Christ. His sermons are deeply passionate and full of entreaties to his hearers. Themes of the judgement of God on sin, the grace of God in sending his son for the redemption of humankind and the mercy of God in Christ Jesus are regular and prominent. But perhaps the clearest expression of Calvin's missionary heart is in the prayers with which he closed his sermons.

---

17. Scott Simmons, *John Calvin and Missions: A Historical Study*, 2003. http://www.aplacefortruth.org/calvin.missions1.htm (accessed 20 October, 2010).

It will be clear from this survey that Calvin was genuinely a man with mission at the centre of his being but let me give the last word to Calvin himself in one of his liturgical prayers:

We pray you now, O most gracious God and merciful Father, for all people everywhere. As it is your will to be acknowledged as the Saviour of the whole world, through the redemption wrought by Your Son Jesus Christ, grant that those who are still estranged from the knowledge of him, being in the darkness and captivity of error and ignorance, may be brought by the illumination of your Holy Spirit and the preaching of your Gospel to the right way of salvation, which is to know You, the only true God, and Jesus Christ whom you have sent.[18]

---

18. Elsie McKee, 'Calvin and praying "for all the people who dwell on earth"', *Interpretation* 63 (April, 2009), 130–140, 139.

CHAPTER 9

'Towards Transformation – Mission in Two Directions': The Perspective of Ignatius Loyola

Laurence J. Murphy

The title of this paper indicates the main themes that will guide this essay. 'Towards' suggests movement, being on a journey, not arriving easily, being a pilgrim, and 'the pilgrim' is how Ignatius Loyola identifies himself in his autobiography.[1] 'Transformation' implies change, making the necessary decisions to bring about change, newness, conversion and reformation. 'Mission' is the key word to understanding the charism of Ignatius and finds its origin in the life of Jesus Christ, the one who was sent. Those who are called to share in the Ignatian charism will contemplate during the *Spiritual Exercises* the life of the One sent and will in turn experience the desire to be sent by the same Lord.

The portrait of Ignatius has been often distorted by a failure to recognise until more recent times what has been revealed as a central feature of his conversion: Ignatius gradually became a mystic who enjoyed what spiritual writers call 'infused

---

1. 'Reminiscences' in *Saint Ignatius of Loyola: Personal Writings*, Translated with introductions and notes by Joseph A. Munitiz and Philip Endean (London: Penguin Books, 1996). Hereafter, this will be cited in the text as *Autobiography*, with reference to the standard paragraph numbers.

contemplation', by which they mean a loving gaze on God, or something pertaining to him, which God produces in a person with his/her cooperation, and which is above what the human intellect, will, or other faculties can produce by their own powers.

THE PILGRIM'S STORY BEGINS

i. Loyola and Montserrat

In a few paragraphs in his *Autobiography*, Ignatius the soldier, wounded in a battle against the French at Pamplona, describes what happened to him when he was carried back with a broken leg to his home in Loyola. Identifying himself as a pilgrim he writes:

> Still, there was this difference: that when he was thinking about that worldly stuff he would take much delight, but when he left it aside after getting tired, he would find himself dry and discontented. But when about going to Jerusalem barefoot, and about not eating except herbs, and about doing all the other rigours he was seeing the saints had done, not only used he be consoled while in such thoughts, but he would remain content and happy even after having left them aside. But he wasn't investigating this, nor stopping to ponder this difference, until one time when his eyes were opened a little, and he began to marvel at this difference in kind and to reflect on it, picking it up from experience that from some thoughts he would be left sad and from others happy, and little by little coming to know the difference in kind of spirits that were stirring: the one from the devil, and the other from God. (*Autobiography*, 8)

In these few lines we have the beginnings of what would become a central element in his way of finding God or being guided by the Spirit and coming to know God's will for him. It remains an essential part of his spirituality: the capacity or grace to become aware of and to understand a little, the difference between the influences working within. Without knowing it, he was linking into an ancient tradition within the Church of 'discerning the spirits'. The first steps towards transformation and conversion had begun and a love affair with the person of Jesus Christ, which in turn evoked in him the desire to go and live in the land where Jesus had lived.

Unfortunately, we cannot delay here to narrate how God was at work in 'the pilgrim' during those seemingly long months of convalescence in Loyola. For the wounded soldier, the tedious hours of recuperation were made bearable by the only books available in the house and they were on the life of Christ and the lives of the saints, books that where to shape his life.

His pilgrimage lead from the family home in Loyola, across northern Spain to the Benedictine monastery at Montserrat in Catalonia, where he kept vigil before the Black Madonna. Ignatius spent three whole days preparing for the confession of the sins of his past life. Then, leaving aside his sword, his dagger and the splendid clothes befitting his former status, he takes himself to Manresa, a small market town lying west of Barcelona.

ii. Manresa

The enduring significance of the eleven months spent in Manresa cannot be exaggerated. Here, surely, was a time of intense learning for the pilgrim. Many years later, dictating his reminiscences to Father da Camera he declares:

> At this time God was dealing with him in the same way as a schoolteacher deals with a child, teaching him. Now, whether this was because of his ignorance and obtuse mind, or because he didn't have anyone to teach him, or because of the resolute will that same God had given him to serve him, it was his clear judgement then, and has always been his judgement, that God was dealing with him in this way. (*Autobiography*, 27)

The time at Manresa can be divided into three phases that may help us to understand better the pilgrim's journey towards gradual change and transformation. It was here, too, that what we today call the *Spiritual Exercises of Saint Ignatius* started to take shape.

The first period was the time of 'first fervour', with days of consolation and much peace. However, he also experienced doubts and temptations: 'And how are *you* going to be able to stand this life the seventy years you are meant to live?' (*Autobiography*, 20) It was a time of penances, vigils, a deliberately slovenly and repulsive exterior, a time of purification and, above all, a surrender to prayer.[2] After three or four months, a second phase began. Things started to change and he lived through a few months of profound turbulence. He describes the rapid alternation of consolations and desolations. Sometimes a deep peace and joy was his to savour, while at other times prayer and liturgies became dry and tasteless. He sought help but found no one. Tortured with scruples he was tempted to take his own life. At times he found himself in peace and then quickly found himself assailed with plaguing questions and doubts. However,

---

2. Pedro Arrupe SJ, *The Trinitarian Inspiration of the Ignatian Charism* (Rome: SJ Press and Information Office; 1980).

when he decided to put these thoughts aside, peace returned. We can see how the pilgrim was being led to a deeper level of understanding the meaning of discernment of spirits. Going beyond the mere awareness of his inner experience, he was beginning to understand and to be able to interpret the meaning of what was happening within himself. A paradigm is taking shape: awareness, understanding, decision to accept or reject.[3]

The third period at Manresa was the most enlightening for the pilgrim, and indeed for us in trying to trace the footsteps of 'the pilgrim': God begins to make his presence felt, with elemental, pictorial representations, acting with him 'as a schoolmaster treats a child whom he is teaching'. These representations have to do with subjects that will be dominant all the rest of his life: the creation of the world, the Eucharist, the humanity of Christ and in the shape of very concrete images, the Trinity.[4] In terms of mission, we can state clearly that Ignatius came to his most profound understanding of mission in the mystery of the Trinity itself. In his own words 'there came to me further understandings, namely how the Son first sent his apostles to preach in poverty, and then the Holy Spirit, giving his spirit and tongues, confirmed them, and thus, the Father and Son sending the Holy Spirit, all three persons confirmed that particular mission'.[5]

3. Timothy M. Gallagher, O.M.V., *The Discernment of Spirits* (New York: Crossroad Publishing Company, 2005), 16–25.

4. Arrupe, paragraph 8.

5. Spiritual Diary of Ignatius, 11 February, 1544. Latin text published in *Monumenta Historica Societatis Jesu*, vol. 63 (Rome, 1934), 86–158. An English translation of the Spiritual Diary is contained in *Saint Ignatius of Loyola: Personal Writings* (cf. footnote 1 above).

iii. The River Cardoner

It was on the banks of the river Cardoner, flowing through Manresa, that Ignatius received his greatest enlightenment:

> Once he was going in his devotion to a church which was a little more than a mile from Manresa (I think it is called St Paul's), and the way goes along by the river. Going along thus in his devotions, he sat down for a little with his face towards the river, which was running deep below. And as he was seated there, the eyes of his understanding began to be opened: not that he saw some vision, but understanding and knowing many things, spiritual things just as much as matters of faith and learning, and this was an enlightenment so strong that all things seemed new to him. One cannot set out the particular things he understood then, though they were many: only that he received a great clarity in his understanding ... And this left him with the understanding enlightened in so great a way that it seemed to him as if he were a different person, and he had another mind, different from that which he had before. (*Autobiography*, 30)

This 'illumination' or mystical experience on the banks of the Cardoner has always been seen as a decisive moment in the life of 'the pilgrim'. The phrase 'all things seemed new to him' had a profound and lasting effect on his life and his way of experiencing all reality. After this experience the pilgrim could see more clearly that God's entry into his life was an invitation that called for a response. God himself was transforming Ignatius. His inner self was being changed, converted, and transformed. Most of all he was finding a *methodology* for all his future change and progress. In the words of Nadal, his confidant, 'there he learned to discern spirits' and again Polanco, his trusted secretary, says: 'that light (received at the Cardoner) had to do concretely with distinguishing good and evil spirits'.[6] While he was in Loyola, Ignatius saw Christ as the eternal king worthy of imitation: now this same Christ was more than a model to be imitated, he was Christ giving a mission to be implemented. Henceforward, Ignatius saw himself as 'a servant of Christ's mission'.

During all this time, the process delineated in the little book called the *Spiritual Exercises* was starting to take shape and appear in the meditations and contemplations presented there. Towards the end of the *Spiritual Exercises* we are guided to contemplate how God dwells in all creatures,

> ... in the elements, giving being, in the plants, causing growth, in the animals producing sensation, and in humankind, granting the gift of understanding – of how he dwells in me, giving me being, life and sensation, and causing me to understand. To see how he makes a temple of me, as I have been created in the likeness and image of his divine majesty.[7]

It was this growing awareness of the presence of God in all creatures, albeit in different ways, that lead him gradually to find God in all things or, expressed in the words of Nadal, to become 'contemplative in action'.

iv. Barcelona, the Holy Land, Alcala and Salamanca

In mid March 1523, 'the pilgrim' leaves Barcelona for the Holy Land where he had intended to stay and preach the gospel of

---

6. Arrupe, op. cit., 20

7. *Spiritual Exercises* (Exx 235), in Saint Ignatius of Loyola, *Personal Writings*.

Jesus. The refusal by the Franciscan provincial to allow him to remain in the Holy Land did not impress 'the pilgrim' until he was told that the same provincial had authority from the Pope to exercise his authority. Some have seen in this act of obedience to the Franciscan provincial the seeds of Ignatius's respect and indeed love of authority as 'the bond of union', which will reappear in his guidelines in the *Spiritual Exercises* for 'thinking and feeling with the Church' and is so evident in the *Constitutions* and letters. His growing desire to 'help souls' underlined his awareness of the need for preparation and study if he was to preach to others, and so this thirty-three year old set about learning Latin in Barcelona. More study and spiritual conversations continued in Alcala and later in Salamanca.

THE PILGRIM'S STORY CONTINUES IN PARIS
In February 1528, Ignatius, now a man of thirty-seven years, entered Paris 'alone and on foot':

> He settled himself in a house with some Spaniards and went to classes in humanities at Montaigu. And the reason for this was that, since they had made him go forward in his studies in such a hurry, he was discovering himself to be very lacking in background. He was studying with the boys, following the structure and method of Paris. (*Autobiography,* 73)

We know that the college of Montaigu was one of the more than fifty colleges that comprised the University of Paris at this time. It had been restored in the late fifteenth century and had a reputation for austerity and discipline. John Calvin had just completed his studies there for the Masters of Arts prior to Ignatius's arrival. The story of the pilgrim's years in Paris is a wonderful account of the life of a poor Basque student who had to beg during the holidays to pay for his studies. His fundraising journeys brought him as far as Flanders and even to London. However, what is perhaps most revealing is to observe how a group of University students from different parts of Europe and from different social backgrounds were attracted to gather round this poor Basque who walked with a limp. Though studies were difficult, he succeeded in his examination for a Licentiate in Arts in March 1533, followed by a Masters of Arts in 1534. All the while he was guiding the others through the experience of the *Spiritual Exercises* so that each in his own time and each in his own way was inspired to follow the poor crucified Christ just as Ignatius himself had been inspired.

On 15 August 1534, these seven companions or 'friends in the Lord' gathered at Montmartre and made vows of poverty and chastity and to go on pilgrimage to Jerusalem 'to spend their lives for the good of souls' there. However, they added another clause: if they could not go to Jerusalem in the space of a year, or could not remain there, 'they would return to Rome and present themselves to Christ's vicar, so that he could employ them wherever he judged to be more for the glory of God and the good of souls'(*Autobiography,* 85). This placing themselves at the service of the Pope, as vicar of Christ, is born out of a profound desire 'to be sent', to be men on a mission from the one who has the care of the universal Church. The 'papal clause' would determine the future of the little group which was taking shape.

The chaotic state of the Church at this time cannot be exaggerated. Confusion, disorientation and the evident need for reform within the Church were everywhere present:

It was enough to live in Paris in that storm of opinions for Ignatius to realise that before putting people face-to-face with Christ in the *Exercises*, he first had to offer some kind of compass to enable them to hold onto their bearings ... He lived in the church, not doubting her. He had no problems with authority or traditional devotions. But now he had to profess his belief in 'holy mother Church' as she really was, as history presented her, a stained Church, the Church 'militant' ... Ignatius believed that the Church, in spite of the weight of the centuries, continued to be 'the true spouse of Christ our Lord'. This was the living principle that animates his *Rules for Thinking with the Church* in the *Exercises*. He believed that one could always find reasons to criticise the Church, but also numerous reasons to defend her. Not that belief must be reduced to blind discipline.[8]

In June 1537, Ignatius and his companions were ordained priests in Venice. He himself, however, would postpone saying his first Mass for one year in order to have time to prepare in the manner he thought best. His love for the Eucharist explains why he is so often portrayed by artists in the vestments of a priest.

THE PILGRIM'S STORY, NO LONGER ALONE, UNFOLDS IN ROME
Finding themselves unable to travel to the Holy Land, three of the companions, Ignatius, Favre and Laynez, set out for Rome to offer their services to Pope Paul III in fidelity to the 'papal clause' of their vow at Montmartre. At the little village of La Storta on the Via Cassia, about sixteen kilometres outside Rome, the pilgrim experienced in prayer one of the most important illuminations of

---

8. Brian Grogan, SJ, *Alone and on Foot: Ignatius Loyola* (Dublin: Veritas, 2009), 116.

his life. In essence, it was a vision of Jesus carrying his cross with God the Father at his side. The Father says to the Son: 'I desire you to take this man as your servant.' Then Jesus says to Ignatius, 'I wish you to serve us' and the Father adds 'I will be propitious to you in Rome.' The overall significance of this illumination for Ignatius lay in seeing himself and his companions being placed with the crucified Christ. This was the answer to the prayer of the 'Two Standards' in the *Spiritual Exercises* where the grace to follow Christ is set against the background of the struggle between evil and good. In that key meditation of the *Spiritual Exercises,* two leaders are presented. Both seek to win over followers employing contrasting and opposing methods. One is led to pray to be received on Christ's side and to recognise the wiles of 'the enemy of human nature'. Later, the opening lines of the papal bull, approving the group as a new religious order echo the words of this illumination at La Storta: 'to serve the Lord alone and the Church his bride, under the Roman Pontiff the Vicar of Christ on earth'. Pope Paul was already beginning to send some of the group on missions to various parts, among them Salmeron and Broet to Ireland as papal delegates.

Faced with this new situation where they could see the little group of friends beginning to disperse, they decided in March 1539 to meet together and to ask themselves two questions. The first question was: should they continue to live in this spiritual friendship with each other or should they simply split up now that the Pope was sending them in different directions? The answer came quickly on the first night: they should continue to be united in spirit. The second question was more complex and no quick answer was arrived at: should they make a vow of obedience to one of themselves? They were fully aware that this was tantamount to forming themselves into a new religious order. On this question, opinions differed and a new manner of reaching a decision as a group was devised. Briefly, this consisted in personal prayer for inner freedom of spirit and light concerning the choice, followed by sharing with the others the fruit of one's prayer. Eventually they decided in the affirmative. This unique act of community discernment would never be repeated in quite the same way, since henceforward there would always be one in the group with the role of leadership. However, the basic methodology of this deliberation is often found to be helpful for groups seeking to reach a decision together. Briefly expressed, this consists in each one praying for freedom of spirit or 'indifference', followed by prayer for light to choose which of the agreed alternatives seems more for the glory of God. Thereupon each shares with the other members of the group what has emerged in their prayer until a consensus is reached.

From late June into July 1539, Ignatius, in consultation with the other companions, wrote the 'Five Chapters' (or a 'Brief Sketch') outlining the nature and purpose of the group which was coming into being and which now needed papal approval. In September of that same year, Pope Paul III gave oral approval to this group of companions which was to become in due time the Company or Society of Jesus. This sketch would be inserted later into a papal document in 1540 (*Regimini Militantis Ecclesiae*) and yet again with some changes in 1550 (*Exposcit Debitum*). For the members of this new group, this document became known as the *Formula of the Institute* and was to serve as the *Regula* or Rule corresponding to the Rule of the older orders, such as the Benedictines or Dominicans.

The new group broke with some of the accepted forms of religious life. There would be no religious habit, no singing of the divine office together in choir, they would form just one community, though broken down into Provinces for administrative purposes, and their apostolate would exclude no ministry where they could be of 'help to souls'. All authority would be centralised in and delegated from the superior general and, perhaps most innovative and controversial in the Roman Curia, the professed members, as well as the traditional vows of poverty, chastity and obedience, would make a solemn vow of obedience to the Pope regarding 'missions'. For Ignatius, this fourth vow was 'our principle and basic foundation' and is the concrete expression of evangelical mission transmitted through the Vicar of Christ.

From 1544 until his death in 1556, Ignatius wrote the *Constitutions* of the nascent Society of Jesus in those small rooms recently restored to their simplicity in the Gèsu in Rome. In these *Constitutions* is contained not so much a code of legal prescriptions but a spirituality for a group of men living in an apostolic community who come together in order to disperse on various missions.[9]

Few Jesuits in recent times have understood the spirit of the Ignatian charism as well as Father Pedro Arrupe, Superior General from 1965 to 1983. In an address delivered in Loyola, Spain, in September 1974, entitled 'Apostolic Mission: Key to the Ignatian Charism', he underlines four Ignatian principles that characterise 'mission'.[10]

The first and highest principle is the primacy of the Divine: 'everything for the greater glory of God' ('*omnia ad maiorem*

---

9. *The Constitutions of the Society of Jesus and their Complementary Norms* (St Louis: The Institute of Jesuit Sources, 1996). Further references to the *Constitutions* will be inserted in text followed by the number.

10. Pedro Arrupe SJ, 'Apostolic Mission: Key to the Ignatiun Charism', *A Planet to Heal* (Rome: Ignatian Centre of Spirituality, 1975), 271–301. This article will henceforth be cited as 'Apostolic Mission'.

Dei gloriam' became the motto of the group). As part of Ignatius's guidelines for novices, he writes in the *Constitutions*: they should often be exhorted to seek God our Lord in all things, removing from themselves as far as possible the love of all creatures in order to place it in the Creator of them, loving him in all creatures and all creatures in him, in conformity with his holy and divine will. (*Constitutions*, 288)

Secondly, Ignatius affirms it is in and by our service of others that God is glorified: 'therefore the human or acquired means ought to be sought with diligence' (*Constitutions*, 814). However:

> ... the means which unite the human instrument with God and so dispose it that it may be wielded well by his divine hand are more effective than those which equip it in relation to human beings. Such means are, for example, goodness and virtue, and especially charity, and a pure intention of the divine service, and familiarity with God our Lord in spiritual exercises of devotion (*Constitutions*, 813).

Thirdly, the ecclesial character of the Ignatian charism is evident in its stated goal of serving the Church under the Roman Pontiff. It is here that the fourth vow of obedience to the Pope enters and where the guidelines for 'thinking with the Church' can be seen in the context of the *Spiritual Exercises*.

Lastly, Arrupe highlights priesthood as a characteristic note of the group as a whole:

> ... this is not to say that all Jesuits must be priests. Rather it says that the Society of Jesus was established for the sake of a labour that pertains to the ministerial priesthood, and so our

work must be the continuance of that experience, at once priestly, personal and communal, of the first companions.[11]

It has been asserted that St Ignatius understood priesthood more in terms of 'the missionary' rather than in terms of 'cult'.

THE MISSION CONTINUES

After cursorily tracing the footsteps of Ignatius 'the pilgrim', and endeavouring to see how he was gradually transformed from being 'a man given up to the vanities of the world ... with a great and vain desire to gain honour' (*Autobiography,* 1) to a Trinitarian mystic able to 'find God in all things', we must ask two questions: first, has Ignatius left any help or guidelines by which others *today* can live in union with Christ in a world different from than that of the sixteenth century? Second, what are the characteristics of those who endeavour to live lives guided by his *Constitutions*?

It was Nadal, his companion, who said of Ignatius that he was '*contemplativus simul in actione*': a contemplative in action. That was a new way of thinking then, perhaps it is still new. Most of us, if we think of a contemplative, probably think of someone who has withdrawn from activity in the world to find God in seclusion. For Ignatius, one can also find God in the midst of activity, hence the phrase which sums up his life and his spirituality: 'to seek and find God in all things'. The advice he gives when asked about the challenge of the spiritual life for those in formation and still engaged in studies is practical and illustrates the Christocentric nature of his spirituality:

---

11. 'Apostolic Mission', 296.

In view of the purpose of our studies, the students cannot devote themselves to long meditations. Over and above the exercises which they have for the acquisition of virtue (namely daily Mass, one hour for prayer and the examen of conscience, and confession and communion every eighth day) they can exercise themselves in seeking the presence of our Lord in all things – for example, in conversing with someone, in walking, looking, tasting, hearing and thinking and everything that they do, since it is true that his Divine Majesty is in all things by his presence, power and essence.[12]

Finding God in all things and in all activities or to become 'a contemplative in action' depended for Ignatius on exercising oneself in seeking God's presence by pausing regularly to become aware of God's presence in the world around and within oneself.[13] Twice a day, whatever he was doing, he would pause for what has been called 'the indispensable prayer'. In that prayer he would deliberately pay attention to the attractions of the good spirit resonating within him as 'spiritual consolation' while becoming alert to the movements caused by the enemy that register as 'spiritual desolation'.

---

12. 'The Mysticism of Saint Ignatius Loyola According to His Spiritual Diary' by Adolf Haas, SJ in *Ignatius of Loyola His Personality and Spiritual Heritage, 1556–1956* (St Louis: The Institute of Jesuit Sources, 1977), 197.

13. Pope Benedict, in his letter to seminarians (18 October 2010): 'That is why it is so important, dear friends that you learn to live in constant intimacy with God. When the Lord tells us to 'pray constantly', he is obviously not asking us to recite endless prayers, but urging us never to lose our inner closeness to God. Praying means growing in this intimacy'. http://www.vatican.va/holy_father/benedict_xvi/letters/2010/documents/hf_ben-xvi_let_20101018_seminaristi_en.html.

In the letter quoted above, the point worth noting is that one must exercise oneself in seeking the presence of our Lord in all things and one can do that throughout the day in the most ordinary activities. In the same letter he continues:

> ... this manner of meditating, by which one finds God our Lord in all things, is easier than trying to elevate ourselves to spiritual things which are more abstract and which require more effort to make them present to ourselves. Furthermore, this splendid exercise will dispose us for great visitations from the Lord, even during a short prayer.

That letter was, of course, directed to those in studies whose days were spent in demanding intellectual activity and whose mental energies needed to be conserved for the task in hand, namely, a solid preparation for future ministry. However, for those who have completed their studies and are now engaged active ministry, Ignatius's insistence on pausing twice a day for fifteen minutes was an indispensable part of his 'pathway to God' and would, I think, be his contribution to 'living in union with Christ in today's world'.

One hesitates to write yet more words about something that one *does*. The Examen Prayer, or 'examen of awareness' or 'examen of consciousness' is an *exercise, a prayer exercise*, but essentially it only happens when one *does* it. Otherwise it is comparable to reading books describing the benefits of physical exercise but never getting round to *doing* some exercise. It is not by chance that Ignatius starts his little book, the *Spiritual Exercises* by comparing 'every method of examining one's conscience, of meditating, contemplating, praying vocally and mentally, and other spiritual activities' to 'strolling, walking and running'.[14] The kind of prayer he suggests here is to help the person praying to follow the Spirit, to be guided by the Spirit. When speaking of Ignatius's docility to the Spirit, Nadal again provides a succinct description: 'with characteristic modesty he would follow the Spirit who was leading, he did not go ahead'.[15] Many adaptations and approaches to this prayer leave ample scope for personal freedom to find what manner or style suits each individual. Like physical exercise, it requires self-discipline and perseverance if it is to bear fruit. Like instructions describing physical exercise, it may feel awkward and constraining at the start but gradually one finds one's own pace and rhythm and may forget the initial instructions.

Ignatius of Loyola was not an innovator. If he can be seen as someone who contributed to knowing how 'to live in union with Christ in today's world', then I believe his main contribution is in two areas already deeply rooted in the life of the Church, namely 'discernment of spirits' and the examination of conscience. It is true that his orderly mind succeeded in inserting both these practices into the *Spiritual Exercises* in a format that makes them accessible or practicable first to the one doing the Exercises but also outside the Exercises with the help of a guide. Our interest here is in understanding how the examen can be linked to the discernment of spirits in the life of any Christian in daily life. If God is truly present in all things, then surely it is worthwhile to pause regularly to become aware of that presence.

In the prayer exercise, one starts by awakening gratitude in becoming aware of the many blessings received in the period under review. It may come as a surprise to the contemporary

---

14. *Spiritual Exercises*, 1.

15. '*Singulari modestia animi, ducentem Spiritum sequebatur, non praeibat*', Nadal, *Dialogi pro Societate* (1560), FN II, 252.

reader to discover how 'gratitude' has come to warrant so much attention in recent years.[16] It is well known that Ignatius commented on how 'ingratitude is the most abominable of sins ... For it is a forgetting of the graces, benefits and blessings received. As such it is the cause, beginning and origin of all sins and misfortunes.'[17] As one prays, one seeks the gift of light from God in order to be able to review the time in the way that God sees it. One passes on to reflect on the time under review. Where has God been present in the events, situations, reactions of the time? Can I arrive at a reflective and discriminating awareness of the movements occurring within me? In other words, has there been 'spiritual consolation' present or was there rather 'spiritual desolation'? It is here, in the regularity of this prayer, that one is *exercising oneself* in the grace-enlightened action of discerning the spirits. Following this third step, I may rejoice to discover how much I have been living under the guidance of the Spirit of God dwelling within me, or on the other hand, I may need to repent when I discover that I have yielded to acting under the influence of the spiritual desolation which was present within me. The prayer concludes by looking forward to the future with renewed trust and hope in God's unconditional love and ongoing guidance. Much has been written on this prayer in recent times that may prove helpful, provided it does not divert from its actual practice![18]

---

16. Cf. *The Psychology of Gratitude,* eds. Robert A. Emmons and Michael E. McCullough (Oxford: Oxford University Press, 2004).

17. *Letters of St Ignatius Loyola,* selected and translated by William J. Young (Chicago: Loyola University Press, 1959), 55.

18. Timothy M. Gallagher, O.M.V., *The Examen Prayer: Ignatian Wisdom for Our Lives Today* (New York: The Crossroad Publishing Company, 2006). David Lonsdale, *Dance to the Music of the Spirit: The Art of Discernment* (London: Darton, Longman and Todd, 1992).

It is this particular prayer practiced regularly that keeps an active person in union with the Spirit of Christ dwelling within and open to the guidance of the same Spirit. In the mind of Ignatius, the same Spirit is alive and guides both those who have authority within the Church and also the other members of Christ's Body: all Christ's disciples are called to be open to the Spirit and to implement the particular mission in life that God has for each one.

Perhaps the second question posed above (what are the characteristics of those who endeavour today to live lives guided by the *Constitutions* written by Ignatius?) is best answered by Paul VI, a Pope who knew first hand both the strengths and the weaknesses of this group:

> In the combination of this fourfold note (religious, apostolic, priestly and united with the Pope by a special bond of love and service) we see displayed all the wonderful richness and adaptability which has characterised the Society during the centuries as those 'sent' by the Church. Hence there have come theological research and teaching, hence the apostolate of preaching, of spiritual assistance, of publications and writings, of the direction of groups, and of formation by means of the Word of God and the Sacrament of Reconciliation. Hence there have come the social apostolate and intellectual and cultural activity which extends from schools for the solid and complete education of youth, all the way to all levels of advanced university studies and scholarly research. Hence the *puerorum ac rudium in christianismo institutio* ('the instruction of children and uneducated in Christian doctrine') which St Ignatius gives to his sons. Hence the missions, a concrete and moving testimony of the

'mission' of the Society. Hence the solicitude for the poor, for the sick, for those on the margins of society. Wherever in the Church, even in the most difficult and extreme fields, in the crossroads of ideologies, in the front line of social conflict, there has been and there is confrontation between the deepest desires of man and the perennial message of the Gospel, there have been and are Jesuits.[19]

Conclusion

Iñigo, or Ignatius as he came to be known, experienced life as a pilgrimage, a continual searching to find God. There can be no doubt that God was guiding this search and allowed 'the pilgrim' to find Him. To those who desire to spend their lives 'living in union with Christ in today's world' the particular way that Ignatius was led to discover is open to others who are ready and willing to engage seriously and generously with the one who was sent and who in turn sends others: Jesus Christ the Lord.

19. Paul VI, 'Address to Thirty-Second General Congregation of the Society of Jesus, December 3 1974', *Documents of the 31st and 32nd General Congregations of the Society of Jesus* (St Louis: The Institute of Jesuit Sources, 1977), 526.

Contributors

Gordon Campbell is Professor of New Testament at Union Theological College, Belfast. Prior to which, he served as a minister in the French Reformed Church and taught at the Faculté Libre de Théologie Réformée at Aix-en-Provence.
His special academic interest is the Book of Revelation, which was the subject of his PhD.

Stafford Carson is a native of Larne. He was brought up in the Elim Pentecostalist tradition. Prior to entering the ministry, he taught science. He served as academic dean at Westminster Theological Seminary. Since 2005, he has been Minister of the First Presbyterian Church, Portadown and served as Moderator of the General Assembly in 2009–2010.

Drew Gibson is Professor of Practical Theology at Union Theological College, Belfast. A native of Belfast, he has served in teaching and pastoral ministry in East Africa.

Tom Layden SJ is a native of Dublin who grew up in Roscommon. He spent twelve years in pastoral work in Belfast. He is currently provincial superior of the Society of Jesus in Ireland.

Brendan McConvery C.Ss.R. is a native of Belfast and a member of the Redemptorist Congregation. He teaches Scripture in the Faculty of Theology, St Patrick's College, Maynooth.

Laurence J. Murphy SJ is a native of Dungannon. He served as director of novices in the Irish Jesuit Province and as Rector of the Collegio Internazionale del Gesù in Rome. He spent six years as Provincial Superior and, since 2005, has been spiritual director of the seminary in Maynooth.

SALVADOR RYAN is a native of Moneygall, which has been made famous recently as the ancestral home of President Barack Obama. He has been professor of Ecclesiastical History at Maynooth since 2008. His research interests lie in the areas of late medieval and early modern popular religion. He lives in Thurles with his wife Michelle and their three children.

LIAM M. TRACEY is a native of Dublin. He is an ordained presbyter of the Order of Friar Servants of Mary (OSM). He did graduate studies in liturgy at the Anselmianum in Rome. He has lectured in Ireland, Australia, Ghana, Italy, United Kingdim and the USA. He is Professor of Liturgy and director of post-graduate studies at the Pontifical University at Maynooth.

STEPHEN N. WILLIAMS is a native of Wales. He has taught in Aberystwyth and Oxford and is currently Professor of Systematic Theology at Union College, Belfast. His publications include *Revelation and Reconciliation: A Window on Modernity* (Cambridge University Press, 1995) and *The Shadow of the Antichrist: Nietzsche's Critique of Christianity* (Baker Academic Press, 2006).

TOM WILSON is Minister of Kilmakee Presbyterian Church, Dunmurry, Co. Antrim. Prior to entering the ministry, he trained in social work and counselling. Since 2000, he has been involved in the ministry of spiritual direction.